Leverage Your Library Program to Help Raise Test Scores:

A Guide for Library Media Specialists, Principals, Teachers, and Parents

Audrey P. Church

Linworth Publishing, Inc.
Worthington, Ohio 43085

Dedication

This book is dedicated to my family,
my friends, and my students,
without whose understanding and encouragement
it would never have been possible.

Library of Congress Cataloging-in-Publication Data

Church, Audrey P., 1957-
    Leverage your library program to help raise test scores : a guide for library media specialists, principals, teachers, and parents / Audrey P. Church.
        p. cm.
    Includes bibliographical references and index.
    ISBN 1-58683-120-8 (perfect bound)
        1. School libraries--United States. 2. Teacher-librarians--United States. 3. Media programs (Education)--United States. 4. Information literacy--United States. 5. Academic achievement--United States. 6. Libraries and education--United States. I. Title.

Z675.S3C5 2003
027.8--dc21

                                                                                    2003040080

Cataloging-in-Publication Data

Published by Linworth Publishing, Inc.
480 East Wilson Bridge Road, Suite L
Worthington, Ohio 43085

Copyright © 2003 by Linworth Publishing, Inc.

ISBN: 1-58683-120-8

5 4 3 2 1

Table of Contents

Table of Contents *continued*

Table of Contents *continued*

Table of Contents *continued*

Acknowledgments

The author wishes to acknowledge the following for their assistance with this book:

- Judi Repman and Alice Yucht, who started me on this book writing adventure

- The reviewers who reviewed the manuscript as it developed and gave invaluable comments and suggestions

- Those administrators, teachers, and library media specialists who testified concerning the difference a strong library program makes within a school

- Pat Levak, Production Manager, Linworth Publishing, for her kind friendship and encouragement

- Donna Miller, Editor, Linworth Publishing, for her thoughtful editorial guidance and assistance

Also, the author wishes to acknowledge those who graciously gave permission for the following material to be quoted and reprinted within:

- *AskERIC* Web page, ERIC Clearinghouse on Information and Technology

- *Boolean Searching on the Internet* Web page, Laura B. Cohen

- *Collaborative Unit Planning Sheet* and *Teacher Library Media Specialist Evaluation of a Collaboratively Taught Unit*, David V. Loertscher

- *EduScapes* Web page, Annette Lamb

- *Good Schools Have School Librarians: Oregon School Librarians Collaborate to Improve Academic Achievement*, Keith Curry Lance

- *A Guide for Elementary School Principals, A Guide for Middle School Principals,* and *A Guide for Secondary School Principals: Academic Success @your Library*, Virginia Department of Education, Office of Educational Technology

- *How School Librarians Help Kids Achieve Standards: The Second Colorado Study*, Keith Curry Lance

- *The Impact of School Library Media Centers on Academic Achievement*, Keith Curry Lance

- *Information Empowered: The School Librarian as an Agent of Academic Achievement in Alaska Schools*, Keith Curry Lance

- *Kentucky Virtual Library* Web page, Kentucky Department of Education

- *KidsConnect KCTools* Web page, American Library Association

- *Make the Connection: Quality School Library Media Programs Impact Academic Achievement in Iowa*, Keith Curry Lance

- *Manchester High School Library Africa Pathfinder*, Lois Harvey Stanton and Catherine Welsh

- *Measuring Up to Standards: The Impact of School Library Programs & Information Literacy in Pennsylvania Schools*, Keith Curry Lance

- *Nine Information Literacy Standards for Student Learning*, American Library Association

- *Prince Edward County Elementary School Library Ancient Greece Pathfinder*, Angela M. Moore

- *Read Across America: The Basics from Start to Finish* Web page, National Education Association

- *School Libraries and MCAS Scores: A Paper Presented at a Symposium Sponsored by the Graduate School of Library and Information Science, Simmons College, Boston, Massachusetts*, James C. Baughman

- *Second Summary: The Hundred Divisions*, OCLC Online Computer Library Center, Inc.

- *Springfield Township High School Library* Web page, Joyce Kasman Valenza

- *SIRS Knowledge Source* Web page, SIRS Publishing, Inc.

- *Texas School Libraries: Standards, Resources, Services, and Students' Performance*, Library Development Division of the Texas State Library

- *Will Hobbs* Web page, Will and Jean Hobbs

Introduction

Neither teachers nor administrators take a basic course in school library media. For many years I have been fascinated by the research studies that show how important school libraries and librarians are to academic achievement and thoroughly frustrated by the fact that very few educators outside of the school library media field are aware of the enormous potential that exists. Moving from a school library setting to a position in higher education has afforded me the opportunity to spread the word within my own small sphere of influence. On my university campus, I frequently speak to administrator preparation classes and to teacher preparation classes, sharing with them information about the role of libraries in today's schools. I present at regional, state, and national conferences. With this book I have the opportunity to truly share the news with an even larger audience.

The purpose of this book is to inform educators (primarily those outside of the field of school library media) of the important role that libraries play in the instructional program of the school and to raise the expectations that these educators have of their school libraries. Written primarily for a non-library audience, the book will explain concrete ways in which the library media specialist, as an instructional partner, can contribute to student learning and achievement. This book will be invaluable to current and future administrators and teachers, parents who want to know more about their child's school, and library media specialists searching for ways to advocate for their programs and to impact student learning.

Everyone in the education field is concerned with test scores. In this time of standards, testing, and accountability, *Leverage Your Library Program to Help Raise Test Scores* explains what other educators can and should expect from their library media specialists and library media programs and provides ideas and resources for library media specialists who are committed to making a difference. Written in "regular education" language as opposed to "libraryese," this book points out what should happen in successful library media programs that are an integral part of the instructional program of the school. It points out what other educators need to know about today's school library media programs and emphasizes the positive effect that strong library media programs have on student learning.

Leverage Your Library Program to Help Raise Test Scores is basically arranged by type of audience. Following this introduction,

Chapter 1 summarizes and reviews the common findings from major research studies that have shown the impact that school librarians and school library programs have on academic achievement. It outlines what strong library media programs should involve, as shown by the research. Chapter 2 addresses what administrators (present and future) should expect from their school libraries. Chapters 3 and 4 discuss what teachers (present and future) should expect from their school libraries. Chapter 5 gives parents an idea of what today's school library is like and what they should expect from a strong library media program. Chapter 6 provides a plan of action, ideas, and resources for library media specialists. Chapter 7 elaborates on the benefits our students will reap from successful efforts by the aforementioned groups and looks at comments by practicing administrators, teachers, and school library media specialists. References and suggested resources for further reading are included at the end of the book. Appendixes include a chronological summary of the research studies, sample planning and unit evaluation forms, sample pathfinders, and principal brochures prepared by the Virginia Department of Education.

Leverage Your Library Program to Help Raise Test Scores is designed to be used by a variety of audiences in a variety of ways. Administrators can use the material to become better informed about today's school library media programs: what they should expect from their library media specialists, what they need to provide in return, and what subsequent gains they might expect in the area of student achievement. Teachers can use it to gain a better understanding of today's teacher-librarian, as library media specialists are called in Canada. They can use it as a springboard for ideas for ways to collaborate instructionally with their library media specialist and raise their children's test scores. Parents can use it to better understand the contributions that a quality library program makes to their children's education. Library media specialists can use it for ideas and resources as well as for an advocacy tool with fellow educators.

On June 4, 2002, First Lady Laura Bush hosted the White House Conference on School Libraries. In her remarks, as reported by the Laura Bush Foundation for America's Libraries, Mrs. Bush noted, "School libraries help teachers teach and children learn . . . Children and teachers need library resources—especially books—and the expertise of a librarian to succeed. Books, information technology, and school librarians who are part of the school's professional team are basic ingredients for student achievement" (1).

The school librarian with the bun, crepe-soled shoes, and polyester suit, shushing students from behind the circulation desk, is no more: today's library media specialist is a teacher-librarian actively involved in the curriculum of the school. Today's library, as Dr. David Loertscher describes in *Reinvent Your School's Library in the Age of Technology,* is "a busy, bustling, learning laboratory" (3).

So, what is all the fuss about? How can you raise your test scores with resources you already have, building on programs and personnel already in place? Read on to find out!

Author Notes:

■ The term "information literacy" is used often in this book. Simply defined, information literacy refers to the ability to recognize a need for information, to access that information, to evaluate it, and to use it.

■ For the sake of readability in this work, all library media specialists are referred to using the male gender.

■ The terms "librarian" and "library media specialist" are used interchangeably.

1

The Research Says...

"Evidence of the positive impact of school librarians on students' academic achievement abounds. Over the past 40 years, dozens of studies conducted throughout the United States and abroad have produced conclusive evidence that this relationship exists," states Dr. Keith Curry Lance, Director of the Colorado-based Library Research Service (Lance et al., *Information Empowered* 8). Since 1993, eight statewide research studies have been done in seven states to document the impact that the school library media program (and all that it entails in this 21st century, information-rich world) has on the academic achievement of students in our K–12 schools:

> Colorado, 1993: *The Impact of School Library Media Centers on Academic Achievement*, Keith Curry Lance, Lynda Welborn, Christine Hamilton-Pennell.

> Alaska, 1999: *Information Empowered: The School Librarian as an Agent of Academic Achievement in Alaska Schools*, Keith Curry Lance, Christine Hamilton-Pennell, Marcia J. Rodney with Lois Peterson and Clara Sitter.

> Pennsylvania, 2000: *Measuring Up to Standards: The Impact of School Library Programs & Information Literacy in Pennsylvania Schools*, Keith Curry Lance, Marcia J. Rodney, Christine Hamilton-Pennell.

> Colorado, 2000: *How School Librarians Help Kids Achieve Standards: The Second Colorado Study*, Keith Curry Lance, Marcia J. Rodney, Christine Hamilton-Pennell.

Massachusetts, 2000: *School Libraries and MCAS Scores: A Paper Presented at a Symposium Sponsored by the Graduate School of Library and Information Science, Simmons College, Boston, Massachusetts*, James C. Baughman.

Oregon, 2001: *Good Schools Have School Librarians: Oregon School Librarians Collaborate to Improve Academic Achievement,* Keith Curry Lance, Marcia J. Rodney, Christine Hamilton-Pennell.

Texas, 2001: *Texas School Libraries: Standards, Resources, Services, and Students' Performance*, prepared for Texas State Library and Archives Commission, Ester G. Smith.

Iowa, 2002: *Make the Connection: Quality School Library Media Programs Impact Academic Achievement in Iowa*, Marcia J. Rodney, Keith Curry Lance, Christine Hamilton-Pennell.

(For more information and further details regarding each of these studies, refer to a chronological analysis found in Appendix A.)

In addition to the research studies, we have data from the 10-year (1988 to 1998) DeWitt Wallace-Reader's Digest funded, Library Power Program, which "concentrated on improving teaching and learning through revitalizing elementary and middle school library media programs in nineteen communities across the country" (Hughes-Hassell and Wheelock 2).

All the data shows that strong library media programs led by strong library media specialists positively impact the academic achievement of students. Where library media specialists collaborate with teachers and take an active role in curriculum and instruction, test scores are higher. Where students learn to locate, evaluate, and use information efficiently and effectively, academic achievement is higher. As Kathleen Kennedy Manzo reports in the March 22, 2000, issue of *Education Week on the Web*, "Among all the states—in which nearly 850 schools were surveyed altogether—scores on state tests improved by 10 points to 15 points in schools with strong library programs and enough qualified staff members" (2). Dr. James Baughman, Professor of Library and Information Science at Simmons College, notes, "A strong body of evidence shows that at all educational levels school libraries directly influence student achievement" (2).

In this chapter, we will take a look at major findings gleaned from the eight statewide studies and the Library Power Program and will examine what the implications are for administrators, teachers, school libraries, school librarians, and student learning. What do we need to see in school libraries to maximize their full potential for educational contributions? The research studies show that the following eight elements should be present:

- A professionally trained, full-time library media specialist

- Adequate support staff

- A strong collection (books, periodicals, and online databases and references) that meets the needs of the school instructional program

- Student access to library resources and information within and beyond the physical library space

- A library media specialist who is knowledgeable about the school curriculum

- A library media specialist who communicates and collaborates with teachers

- A library media specialist who assists teachers in using information technology

- A library media specialist who teaches students information literacy skills

While these attributes are interrelated, we will look at them individually, examining the first four as somewhat quantitative items, capable of being measured, and the final four in more of a qualitative framework.

A PROFESSIONALLY TRAINED, FULL-TIME LIBRARIAN

To have a strong library media program that positively impacts student learning, a school needs a professionally trained, full-time library media specialist. The original Colorado study, published in 1993, noted that students from schools with well-staffed libraries scored higher on the norm-referenced tests than students in schools with fewer library staff (Lance, Welborn, and Hamilton-Pennell 92). The study also found that library media centers that "have more endorsed staff tend to have staff who spend more time identifying materials for instructional units developed by teachers and more time collaborating with teachers in developing such units" (Lance, Welborn, and Hamilton-Pennell 39). The 1999 Alaska study concluded that a school should have a professionally trained, full-time library media specialist. "Where there is a librarian, test scores are higher. Generally, a school with a full-time librarian has higher test scores than a school with a part-time librarian. Accordingly, a school with a part-time librarian is likely to have higher test scores than a school with no librarian" (Lance et al. 66). The 2000 Pennsylvania study concludes that "each library should have at least one, full-time certified school librarian with at least one full-time aide or other support staff member . . . The relationship between such staffing and PSSA [Pennsylvania System of School Assessment] reading scores is both positive and statistically significant" (Lance, Rodney, and Hamilton-Pennell, *Measuring Up* 35).

The second Colorado study findings, published in 2000, show that "in promoting high academic achievement, the success of any LM [library media] program depends on the presence of adequate staffing— at least one full-time, licensed library media specialist (LMS) with at least one full-time aide or other support staff" (Lance, Rodney, and Hamilton-Pennell, *How School Librarians Help Kids* 39). Likewise, the 2000 Massachusetts study notes, "At the elementary and high school levels, students who are served by a full-time school librarian have higher MCAS [Massachusetts Comprehensive Assessment System] scores than those in schools without a full-time librarian" (Baughman 9). Evidence of this need was so strong in Oregon that it impacted the title assigned to the published study, *Good Schools Have School Librarians*. The 2001 Oregon study notes that "a strong LM [library media] program is one that is adequately staffed . . . Minimally this means one full-time library media specialist (LMS) and one full-time aide" (Lance, Rodney, and Hamilton-Pennell, *Good Schools* 84). Similarly, findings from the 2001 Texas study state that "the Texas Study demonstrated higher TAAS [Texas Assessment of Academic Skills] performance at all educational levels in schools with librarians than in schools without librarians" (Smith 1). The 2002 Iowa study concludes that "in promoting high academic achievement, the success of any library media (LM) program depends on the presence of at least one full-time, professionally-trained and credentialed library media specialist" (Rodney, Lance, and Hamilton-Pennell 39).

Having a trained, full-time library media specialist, then, is critical to the potential impact that the library program has on academic achievement.

ADEQUATE SUPPORT STAFF

In addition to having a professional library media specialist, the research shows consistently that adequate support staff is critical. Having support staff frees the library media specialist from clerical duties to perform instructional duties that impact student learning.

The 1993 Colorado study notes: "The size of a library media center's staff and collection is the best school predictor of academic achievement" (Lance, Welborn, and Hamilton-Pennell 92). More staff translates to more services, which then positively impacts test scores. The Pennsylvania study concludes that "each library should have at least one full-time certified school librarian with at least one full-time aide or other support staff member . . . The relationship between such staffing and PSSA reading scores is both positive and statistically significant" (Lance, Rodney, and Hamilton-Pennell, *Measuring Up* 35). The second Colorado study findings show that "in promoting high academic achievement, the success of any LM [library media] program depends on the presence of adequate staffing—at least one full-time, licensed library media specialist (LMS) with at least one full-time aide or other support staff" (Lance, Rodney, and Hamilton-Pennell, *How School Librarians Help Kids* 39). The Massachusetts study notes that "at the elementary and high school levels, library staff assistance (non-professional help) makes a positive difference in average MCAS scores" (Baughman 9). The Oregon study notes that "a strong LM [library media] program is one that is adequately staffed . . . Minimally, this means one full-time library media specialist (LMS) and one full-time aide" (Lance, Rodney, and Hamilton-Pennell, *Good Schools* 84). The Iowa study reaches the same conclusion: "a strong LM [library media] program is one that is adequately staffed . . . Minimally, this means one full-time library media specialist (LMS) and one full-time aide" (Rodney, Lance, and Hamilton-Pennell 74).

The presence of library support staff makes a positive difference in student academic achievement because it allows the library media specialist to take a more active role in instruction.

A STRONG LIBRARY COLLECTION

In addition to library personnel (a professional library media specialist and support staff), the research demonstrates the need for a strong library collection (books, periodicals, and online databases and references) that meets the needs of the instructional program of the school. The original Colorado study notes that students from schools with strong collections scored higher on the norm-referenced tests than students in schools with weaker collections (Lance, Welborn, and Hamilton-Pennell 92). The second Colorado study reports that "CSAP [Colorado Student Assessment Program] reading test scores increase with . . . print volumes per student, periodical subscriptions per 100 students, [and] electronic reference titles per 100 students (7th grade)" (Lance, Rodney, and Hamilton-Pennell, *How School Librarians Help Kids* 77). The Massachusetts study notes, "At each grade level, students score higher on MCAS tests when there is a higher per pupil book count" (Baughman 8). The Oregon study reports:

> Oregon reading test scores increase with increases in total staff hours per 100 students (including both professional and support staff), print volumes per student, periodical subscriptions per 100 students, and library media expenditures per student. Whatever the current level of development of a school's library media program, these findings indicate that incremental improvements in its staffing, collections, and budget will yield incremental increases in reading scores (Lance, Rodney, and Hamilton-Pennell, *Good Schools* 83).

In the Texas study, library variables found to be important at the elementary school level included library volumes purchased per 100 students and library software packages per 100 students. At the high school level they included volumes per student and current subscriptions to periodicals per 100 students (Smith 2). The Iowa study reports that reading test scores in grades four, eight, and eleven are positively impacted by the size of the collection and the availability and accessibility of the collection to students (Rodney, Lance, and Hamilton-Pennell 42–44).

Better collections of quality materials positively impact test scores.

STUDENT ACCESS TO LIBRARY RESOURCES BOTH WITHIN AND OUTSIDE OF LIBRARY WALLS

S imply having a large collection of quality materials is not sufficient. We must provide access to these resources. Access involves libraries that are open and accessible to students at the time of need. It also involves making electronic information resources available not only in the library but also in computer labs and classrooms within the school and remotely from students' homes.

The Alaska study reports that "higher levels of librarian staffing lead to longer LMC [library media center] hours of operation, higher levels of library media staff activity, higher student usage, and consequently, higher test scores" (Lance et al. 66) and that "test scores also tend to be higher where . . . the library media program provides online access to information—particularly the facilities required to reach the Internet and the World Wide Web" (Lance et al. 67). The Pennsylvania study notes that "where networked computers link school libraries with classrooms, labs, and other instructional sites, students earn higher PSAA reading test scores. These higher scores are particularly linked to the numbers of computers enabling teachers and students to utilize the ACCESS PENNSYLVANIA database, licensed databases, and Internet/World Wide Web" (Lance, Rodney, Hamilton-Pennell, *Measuring Up* 57).

This finding is reinforced in the second Colorado study, which notes, "Where networked computers link library media centers with classrooms, labs, and other instructional sites, students earn higher CSAP reading test scores. These higher scores are particularly linked to the numbers of computers enabling teachers and students to utilize LMC resources, either within the LMC or networked to the LMC, licensed databases, and Internet/World Wide Web" (Lance, Rodney, and Hamilton-Pennell, *How School Librarians Help Kids* 77). The Massachusetts study notes that "at each grade level, hours open make a difference in MCAS scores" (Baughman 8) and that "at each grade level, student use of the library produces higher mean MCAS scores" (Baughman 8). In the Texas study, library hours of operation per 100 students were found to be important at the high school level (Smith 2). The Iowa study concludes:

> A strong LM [library media] program is one that embraces networked information technology. The library media center of today is no longer a destination; it is a point of departure for accessing the information resources that are the essential raw material of teaching and learning. Computers in classrooms, labs and other school locations provide networked access to information resources—the library catalog, electronic full text, licensed databases, locally mounted databases. Students succeed where the LM program is not a place to go, apart from other sites of learning in the school, but rather an integral part of the educational enterprise that reaches out to students and teachers where they are" (Rodney, Lance, and Hamilton-Pennell ix).

Providing access to information resources, both within and outside of the school library, at the point of need, positively impacts student achievement.

      Thus far in this chapter we have discussed quantitative items. Does the school have a professional, full-time library media specialist assisted by support staff? Does the school library have an adequate collection of materials and resources? Are these resources, print and electronic, available for students to use? Each of these questions may be answered with a "yes" or a "no." Those schools that answer "yes" are on their way to higher test scores. The next four items refer to activities. They refer to usage of these materials. They require a library media specialist who is willing to take resources and use them productively for student learning. They require a more qualitative assessment of the library media program.

A LIBRARY MEDIA SPECIALIST WHO IS KNOWLEDGEABLE ABOUT SCHOOL CURRICULUM

It is imperative that today's library media specialist be knowledgeable about the school's curriculum. As the research studies show, when this is the case, students benefit. The Pennsylvania study notes that "test scores increase as school librarians spend more time serving on standards committees and serving on curriculum committees" (Lance, Rodney, and Hamilton-Pennell, *Measuring Up* 58). The Massachusetts study shows that "at the elementary level, students score higher on the MCAS tests when the library is aligned with the state curriculum frameworks. (This fact is especially true in schools that have a high percentage of free school lunches—the socioeconomic factor)" (Baughman 9). The Oregon study reports that "a strong LM [library media] program is one whose staff are involved leaders in their school's teaching and learning enterprise. A successful LMS [library media specialist] is one who . . . serves with other teachers on the school's standards and curriculum committees" (Lance, Rodney, and Hamilton-Pennell, *Good Schools* xi). The Iowa study reports similar findings: "A strong LM [library media] program is one whose staff are involved leaders in their school's teaching and learning enterprise. A successful LMS is one who . . . serves with other teachers on the school's standards and curriculum committees" (Rodney, Lance, and Hamilton-Pennell ix).

      Knowledge of the curriculum allows the library media specialist to purchase appropriate resources for the collection and to connect library instructional activities with the curriculum. It is important that the library media specialist participate on curriculum committees and have a working knowledge of the school's curriculum.

A LIBRARY MEDIA SPECIALIST WHO COMMUNICATES AND COLLABORATES WITH TEACHERS

For the library media specialist to impact student achievement, he must communicate with teachers, meet to cooperatively plan instructional units, and collaborate with teachers for instruction. When the library media specialist takes an active role in the instructional program of the school, test scores rise.

The original Colorado study notes that "the instructional role of the library media specialist shapes the collection and, in turn, academic achievement" (Lance, Welborn, and Hamilton-Pennell 92). The Alaska study states, "The higher the level of librarian staffing, the greater the percentage of library media staff hours devoted to planning instructional units cooperatively with teachers . . . Regardless of level of librarian staffing, the more library media staff time devoted to these activities, the higher the test scores" (Lance et al. 66). The Pennsylvania study reports that "test scores increase as school librarians spend more time teaching cooperatively with teachers" (Lance, Rodney, and Hamilton-Pennell, *Measuring Up* 58). According to the second Colorado study, "test scores rise in both elementary and middle schools as library media specialists and teachers work together . . . Test scores increase as library media specialists spend more time planning cooperatively with teachers (7th grade), identifying materials for teachers" (Lance, Rodney, and Hamilton-Pennell, *How School Librarians Help Kids* 78).

The Oregon study shows that "a strong LM [library media] program is one whose staff have collegial, collaborative relationships with classroom teachers. A successful LMS is one who works with a classroom teacher to identify materials that best support and enrich an instructional unit" (Lance, Rodney, and Hamilton-Pennell, *Good Schools* 84). In Texas, a library variable found to be important at the middle school level was "identifying materials for instructional units developed by teachers" and at the high school level, "planning instructional units with teachers" (Smith 2). The Iowa study echoes the Oregon findings: "A strong LM [library media] program is one whose staff have collegial, collaborative relationships with classroom teachers. A successful LMS is one who works with a classroom teacher to identify materials that best support and enrich an instructional unit" (Rodney, Lance, and Hamilton-Pennell ix).

When the library media specialist serves as a collaborative, instructional partner with classroom teachers, test scores rise.

A LIBRARY MEDIA SPECIALIST WHO ASSISTS TEACHERS IN USING INFORMATION TECHNOLOGY

When the library media specialist provides inservice training to teachers in the effective use of information technology, academic achievement is higher. The Alaska study notes: "The higher the level of librarian staffing, the greater the percentage of library media staff hours devoted to providing in-service training to teachers and other staff. Regardless of level of librarian staffing, the more library media staff time devoted to these activities, the higher the test scores" (Lance et al. 68). The Pennsylvania study reports that "test scores increase as school librarians spend more time providing in-service training to teachers and managing information technology" (Lance, Rodney, and Hamilton-Pennell, *Measuring Up* 58). The second Colorado study points out that "scores also increase with the amount of time library media specialists spend as in-service trainers of other teachers, acquainting them with the rapidly changing world of information. Test scores increase as library media specialists spend more time providing in-service training for teachers, managing a computer network through which the library media program reaches beyond its own walls to classrooms, labs, and offices (7th grade)" (Lance, Rodney, and Hamilton-Pennell, *How School Librarians Help Kids* 78). The Oregon study notes that "a successful LMS is one who is a provider of inservice training opportunities to classroom teachers" (Lance, Rodney, and Hamilton-Pennell, *Good Schools* 84). In the Texas study, a library variable found to be important at the high school level was "providing staff development to teachers" (Smith 2). Again, the Iowa study confirms that "a successful LMS is one who is a provider of inservice training opportunities to classroom teachers" (Rodney, Lance, and Hamilton-Pennell ix).

To positively impact test scores, the library media specialist should train teachers in the use of information technology: online catalogs, licensed databases, and the Internet.

A LIBRARY MEDIA SPECIALIST WHO TEACHES STUDENTS INFORMATION LITERACY SKILLS

It is critical in this information age that we help our students become information literate—able to access, evaluate, and use information. This teaching responsibility belongs to the library media specialist. When the library media specialist teaches information literacy skills in conjunction with classroom content, student achievement and test scores are higher.

The Alaska study reports the following findings: "The higher the level of librarian staffing, the greater the percentage of library media staff hours devoted to delivering library/information literacy instruction to students. Regardless of level of librarian staffing, the more library media staff time devoted to these activities, the higher the test scores" (Lance et al. 66). "The more often students receive library/information literacy instruction in which library media staff are involved, the higher the test scores" (Lance et al. 66). The Pennsylvania study notes that "the 'keystone' finding of this study is the importance of an integrated approach to information literacy. For school library programs to be successful agents of academic achievement, information literacy must be an integral part of the school's approach to both standards and curriculum. Test scores increase as school librarians spend more time teaching cooperatively with teachers and teaching information literacy independently" (Lance, Rodney, and Hamilton-Pennell, *Measuring Up* 57–58).

The second Colorado study reports that "a central finding of this study is the importance of a collaborative approach to information literacy. Test scores rise in both elementary and middle schools as library media specialists and teachers work together. Test scores increase as library media specialists spend more time . . . teaching information literacy skills to students" (Lance, Rodney, and Hamilton-Pennell, *How School Librarians Help Kids* 78). The Massachusetts study notes that "at the elementary and middle/junior high school levels, students score higher on the MCAS tests when there is a library instruction program" (Baughman 9). The Oregon study reports that "a strong LM [library media] program is one whose staff have collegial, collaborative relationships with classroom teachers. A successful LMS is one who . . . is a teacher of essential information literacy skills to students" (Lance, Rodney, and Hamilton-Pennell, *Good Schools* 84). In Texas a library variable found to be important at the middle school level was "providing information skills instruction to individuals or groups" (Smith 2). The Iowa study confirms the Oregon findings: "A strong LM [library media] program is one whose staff have collegial, collaborative relationships with classroom teachers. A successful LMS [library media specialist] is one who . . . is a teacher of essential information literacy skills to students" (Rodney, Lance, and Hamilton-Pennell ix).

It is critically important that library media specialists teach students information literacy skills and that these skills be taught, not separately in isolation, but in conjunction with regular classroom content material. When this type of instruction occurs, test scores go up.

NATIONAL LIBRARY POWER PROGRAM: A MAJOR INITIATIVE OF THE DEWITT WALLACE-READER'S DIGEST FUND

Library Power was a ten-year (1988–1998), $40 million initiative funded by the DeWitt Wallace-Reader's Digest Fund. It impacted elementary and middle school library media programs in 19 communities across the country, operating in approximately 700 schools and affecting more than 400,000 students.

The Library Power Program had six National Program Goals as explained on the American Association of School Librarians' Web site at <http://www.ala.org/aasl/libpower/index.html>:

- To create a national vision and new expectations for public elementary and middle school library programs and to encourage new and innovative uses of the library's physical and human resources

- To create exemplary models of library media programs that are an integral part of the educational process

- To strengthen the role of the librarian as a teacher, information specialist and learning facilitator who assists teachers and students in becoming effective users of ideas and information

- To encourage collaboration among teachers, administrators, and librarians that results in significant improvement in teaching and learning processes

- To demonstrate the significant contributions that library programs can make to school reform and restructuring efforts

- To encourage the creation of partnerships among leaders in school districts, public libraries, community agencies, business communities, academic institutions, and parent groups to improve and support school library programs

In Library Power schools, library facilities were renovated and refurbished. Professionally trained library media specialists, if not already in place, were hired. Collections were augmented and updated. Flexible access and flexible scheduling were implemented so that students and teachers had access to library professionals and resources at the point of need. Administrative, teacher, and community understanding of and support for school library media programs was developed. Library media specialists took an active role in the instructional program of their schools, collaborating with teachers and working with students to develop information literacy skills.

Evaluation of the Library Power Program shows that school library media programs play an important part in teaching and learning. Benefits include better facilities and stronger collections, and the program helps "schools engage students in meaningful and educationally rich learning activities" (Wheelock 5). In summary, "Library Power demonstrates how schools can effectively use library resources and practices to promote a shared curriculum and contribute powerfully to improve instruction" (Wheelock 23).

IN CONCLUSION . . .

It is important to note that the findings from numerous statewide studies conducted in states as geographically and culturally diverse as Alaska, Colorado, Iowa, Massachusetts, Oregon, Pennsylvania, and Texas and from the Library Power project all demonstrate the impact that school libraries have on academic achievement. "Studies demonstrate consistently that well-equipped, quality school library media centers that have professional staff involved in instruction contribute to the academic success of their students" (Lance, Rodney, and Hamilton-Pennell, *Good Schools* 24). You have the potential to raise your students' test scores by effectively utilizing your school library — no outside consultants needed, no software programs to purchase, no major educational reform movements to implement. Leveraging your library media program to maximize its potential will positively impact students' test scores.

Of course, we recognize that many factors may influence student achievement and test scores: the economic level of the community in which the school is located, the amount of funding the school receives, the educational level of students' parents, the importance placed on educational achievement in the home, and the socioeconomic levels from which the students come. The research studies discussed previously analyzed school differences and community differences, and it is noted: "The impact of LM [library media] program development on academic achievement cannot be explained away by: school differences, including school district expenditures per pupil, teacher/pupil ratio, the average years of experience of classroom teachers, and their average salaries; or community differences, including adult educational attainment, children in poverty, and racial/ethnic demographics" (Lance, Rodney, and Hamilton-Pennell, *Good Schools* x). All the empirical data collected points to the positive impact a strong library media program can have on student achievement.

Take a close look at your school library media program and your school library media specialist. The resources that you need are already in place. You just need to read on to find out how to tap into and maximize the tremendous potential that is there!

2

What Administrators Should Know and Expect

I f you presently serve as a school principal, supervisor, director, or superintendent, you have been a classroom teacher. If you are currently enrolled in a principal preparation/educational leadership program, chances are that you are a classroom teacher. In either case, at some stage in your educational career, you have taught in the classroom. While the point has been made that a career in school library media provides natural preparation for administrative positions (Pennock 117), very few administrators have actually been school library media specialists. While you, as an administrator, know what to expect from a classroom teacher, you may not have a good idea of what to expect from your library media specialist. Take the following pretest to check your knowledge.

ADMINISTRATORS' PRETEST

Respond to each of the following statements by answering true *or* false.

My librarian

1. concerns himself with content area standards.
2. actively participates in curriculum development.
3. promotes reading.
4. meets, plans, and collaborates with classroom teachers.
5. teaches students how to access, evaluate, and use information.
6. trains teachers in the use of information technology.
7. promotes ethical and responsible use of information.
8. takes an active role in the instructional program of the school.
9. effectively manages the library collection and library program to make it an integral part of the school.

Did you answer *true* to each of these statements? If so, you are an administrator in a school that has a strong librarian and a strong library media program. If you weren't able to answer affirmatively to all of them, did any of them surprise you? Are these activities that you, as an administrator, expect of your library media specialist? Activities such as these make a difference in student achievement.

What does the library media specialist do all day? What is this person supposed to do all day? How does he fit into the total instructional program of the school? What should you expect? If you do find all the following characteristics in your library media specialist and the following elements in your school library media program, what can you realistically expect as the result? Let's take a look at collaboration, information literacy, information technology, reading promotion, program administration, and leadership.

COLLABORATION

Library media specialists of the 21st century are no longer isolated "keepers of the books." Today's library media specialists are called upon to be full-fledged instructional partners actively involved in the total instructional program of the school (*Information Power* 4–5). For numerous reasons, they must be well-versed in the curriculum and in content area standards in place in your school, your school district, and your state.

First, the library media specialist must be totally cognizant of content area standards in order to purchase resources that support the instructional program of the school. If students are studying Ancient China at the third grade level, the library media specialist searches for appropriate fiction and nonfiction books related to Ancient China. He may find an excellent instructional video about the early dynasties presented at just the appropriate level. When middle school students are studying basic documents central to United States history in civics class, such as the *Declaration of Independence*, *Articles of Confederation*, and *Constitution of the United States*, the library media specialist works to have not only the text of these primary source documents but also interpretations and explanations appropriate for middle school students. If high school biology students study photosynthesis, the library media specialist searches for quality nonfiction books to provide the teacher with additional information and to provide the students with information resources for research. He also may purchase an interactive software program that will help students master this content.

Second, the library media specialist's awareness of content area standards allows him to reinforce what is happening instructionally in the classroom. Particularly at the elementary school level, library media specialists have the opportunity to reinforce concepts from the classroom in the library setting. For example, if third grade students are working with decimals and place value in mathematics, this is an excellent opportunity for real-life reinforcement of the concept. The library media specialist explains the Dewey decimal system and shelving of nonfiction books using those very same mathematical principles. If fifth grade students are working on the concept of classification of plants and animals in science, the perfect opportunity presents itself for the library media specialist to teach and share the concept of classification of library materials. In these situations, the library media specialist is not only aware of the content standards and willing to make connections to them, but is also in communication with content area teachers to coordinate instruction.

Third, with a thorough knowledge of content area standards and a willingness to partner with classroom teachers, the library media specialist can serve as a fully collaborative instructional partner. He is available to plan, teach collaboratively, and co-evaluate with classroom teachers. When grade level teachers, teams of teachers, or departments of teachers meet, the library media specialist meets with them to plan. The library media specialist also willingly plans with individual teachers on a one-to-one basis. Library instruction is totally integrated into the classroom content lessons. When students are studying alphabetizing by the first letter of the word in their first grade classroom, in the library they are discussing how fiction books are arranged in alphabetical order on the shelves by the first letter of the author's last name.

Many classroom assignments require the use of library information resources. Information-seeking is a natural, integral part of the assignment. Both the library media specialist and the classroom teacher, as instructional partners, teach portions of the lesson and evaluate the students' products. Take, for example, a collaborative research project involving eleventh graders in which the classroom teachers in English and United States history partner with the library media specialist. The English and history teachers decide to collaborate on a major assignment for the year—research project/term paper/oral presentation—and realize that the library media specialist is a natural partner for the endeavor. Students will choose a topic that they have discussed in history class about which they are curious and want to learn more. The library media specialist will assist the students in narrowing their topics, will teach them to evaluate information sources critically, will remind them to properly credit sources, and will assist them with the presentation software as they prepare their oral presentations. When assessment time arrives, the library media specialist can take an active part, evaluating the quality of the information sources students used and perhaps grading the works cited. The history teacher may focus her assessment on content, and the English teacher may focus his assessment on the writing elements. Any or all of these instructional partners may grade the students' oral presentations and collaboratively assign the final grade.

A note here: classroom teachers, in most instances, are not accustomed to partnering with library media specialists for instruction. They tend to view the library media specialist as a resource person or in the reinforcement role. You as the administrator need to promote and support this collaborative instructional culture. A library media specialist ready to collaborate and teachers ready to partner make powerful instructional teams.

Does this collaborative instructional model make a difference in test scores? Is it "worth the teacher's time" to partner with the library media specialist for instruction? Faye Pharr, Principal of Lakeside Academy of Math, Science, and Technology, Chattanooga, Tennessee, shared this statistic at the June 4, 2002, White House Conference on School Libraries:

> After the first year of flexible scheduling, with all library projects based on teacher/librarian collaboration, we found there was direct correlation between library usage and improved test scores. After running the end-of-the-year circulation report, it became obvious that the teachers who had the highest library usage also had the highest test scores. A detailed analysis revealed there was a direct link between library usage and test scores in the reference study and reading comprehension. For example, the classroom with the highest library usage had a mastery percentage of 86% in reference study and 81% in comprehension. The teacher who offered the most resistance to collaborative planning and library usage also had the lowest in mastery scores—19% in reference study and 52% in comprehension (Laura Bush Foundation 3).

INFORMATION LITERACY

Information literacy is defined as the ability to access information efficiently and effectively, to evaluate information critically and competently, and to use information accurately and creatively (*Information Power* 8). It is the responsibility of the library media specialist to ensure that students acquire these skills—skills that are critically important in this information age and critically important for creating independent users/learners.

As students work to access and find information, for academic or personal pursuits, the library media specialist teaches them the skills needed to access information efficiently and effectively. He helps them to construct focused questions that will direct the research. He teaches them to identify the various possible sources of information (encyclopedia, book, periodical, Web site) and to select the best source for that particular information need. He teaches them to use Boolean logic to broaden or narrow a search in an electronic database or on the World Wide Web.

Next the library media specialist teaches the students to evaluate the information found. Does it meet the information need? Does it answer the questions set forth? Is the information from an appropriate source? Is the information authoritative, accurate, unbiased, and current? These are questions that the students need to ask if they are to become critical consumers of information.

Finally, the library media specialist assists the students in using the information to develop an authentic, creative product. Here communication and collaboration with the classroom teacher is key. When the assignment is developed, if the library media specialist is a contributing, instructional partner, he can suggest alternative products to the classroom teacher. Rather than the traditional three-to-five page report, perhaps a more appropriate product for an assignment would be a brochure, a newsletter, or an oral presentation.

Examples for different levels follow.

ELEMENTARY

Access: Language arts standards require that our fifth grade students write to inform and to explain. They need to synthesize information from a variety of sources, develop notes, organize and record information, use available electronic databases, and credit secondary reference sources. Science standards require that students investigate and understand characteristics of the ocean environment (*Standards of Learning* 67, 42).

After collaboratively planning with the library media specialist, the fifth grade teacher asks students to select and research an ocean creature. In the school's computer lab, students access the ocean article in an online encyclopedia, reading general information about the ocean and its inhabitants. One student is fascinated by starfish, another by the octopus, and a third by the blue crab. Students make their topic choices, and the classroom teacher discusses with them a graphic organizer that she and the library media specialist have developed to facilitate note taking. Students are required to use at least three different types of information sources.

continued

At this point, the students go to the library to begin gathering information. The library media specialist reviews with them sources of information that they have learned to use previously: encyclopedias, nonfiction books located using the online catalog, magazine articles found in the electronic database, and appropriate search tools to locate Web sites. He reviews the questions on their graphic organizer and reminds them to write down the sources of their information.

Evaluate: Our octopus researcher discovers that the library does not have any books on her creature. She does find a good bit of information in the online encyclopedia, however, and a very informative magazine article from *Ranger Rick* in the periodical database. When she does a Web search, she locates the Web site of the National Aquarium in Baltimore at <http://www.aqua.org> and decides that this is an authoritative site to use. One by one, she uses these sources and takes notes on her graphic organizer, noting carefully what information comes from what source, since both the teacher and the library media specialist require her to turn in a bibliography.

Use: Students compose and word process their research reports, assisted by both the teacher and the library media specialist. All the reports are then compiled into one book on ocean creatures, which is bound and placed in the library collection.

MIDDLE

Access: Our middle school students, in their study of the solar system, are required to complete a research project. Each student selects a planet. The teacher requires each student to find 10 facts about his or her planet. The teacher and the library media specialist have met and discussed the assignment and its requirements, and the library has adequate resources in place. The student is allowed to use general reference works, nonfiction works, periodical articles, and the Internet, always citing sources. The final product will be a travel brochure, promoting a trip to the planet, and must include a picture or two.

Evaluate: Our sixth grader starts with an encyclopedia article to find general information about his chosen planet, Saturn. The library media specialist introduces him to a specialized science reference source, Grolier's *New Book of Popular Science*, where he finds an excellent article that gives all sorts of facts about Saturn. Next, he checks out *Saturn* by Elaine Landau (Franklin Watts, 1999) from the 500 section of the library and reads it to find interesting facts. Finally, he visits a Web site that his

continued

teacher has suggested: Bill Arnett's *The Nine Planets: A Multimedia Tour of the Solar System* at <http://seds.lpl.arizona.edu/nineplanets/nineplanets/nineplanets.html>. Here he must evaluate the information he finds to be sure that he is focused on and taking notes about his planet, Saturn.

Use: Having researched and organized his information, our sixth grader now works with the teacher and the library media specialist to develop his travel brochure using a desktop publishing program. He lists his 10 facts and illustrates them with photos, encouraging his fellow students to book a vacation travel adventure to Saturn. He credits all the sources he has used.

SECONDARY

Access: In our eleventh grade illustration, a student may be very interested in the time period after World War II, the time period named the Cold War. The library media specialist can help the student narrow his topic and develop focused questions to structure his research. As the student reads and explores, he decides to focus his investigation and report on the Berlin Wall—what led to its construction, why it was constructed in 1961, what it meant to the people in Germany and to the world, and why it came down in 1989. The library media specialist then points the student to library reference works, appropriate nonfiction books, periodical databases, and quality Web sites. He helps the student construct effective search strategies for electronic resources, for example, "Berlin AND Wall AND Kennedy," for information focusing on John F. Kennedy's role in this time period, and "Berlin AND Wall AND fall" for information dealing with the bringing down of the Wall in 1989.

Evaluate: Our Berlin Wall researcher must evaluate the information that he has found to be sure that it is relevant to his research. He must, as Jamie McKenzie says, "sort and sift" (72). Next, our researcher must evaluate the appropriateness of his resource. Is a general encyclopedia acceptable, or should he look at a specialized reference source? Is the book by Doris M. Epler entitled *The Berlin Wall: How It Rose and Why It Fell* (Millbrook, 1992) a good source? Is the Web site, *Berlin Wall* at <http://www.wall-berlin.org/> an accurate, authoritative, unbiased site?

Use: Our researcher's teachers originally thought to require a written report but, after planning with the library media specialist, were agreeable to alternate products in addition to the assigned oral presentation. Our student decides to do front pages of a newspaper for 1961 and for 1989 with all the news on the page presenting information about his event. The student must organize and synthesize the information he has gathered. The

continued

library media specialist can assist as the student credits his sources and prepares his newspapers and presentation. Pictures used with permission from Web sites can be inserted into the products and will add greatly to their authenticity. The student may even use a brief snippet of music from the early 1960s to open the oral presentation and a snippet from the late 1980s to close.

Throughout the research process, the library media specialist actively teaches the students to access, evaluate, and use information effectively. In the context of the classroom content and assignment, the library media specialist helps the students gain critical information literacy skills.

INFORMATION TECHNOLOGY

Technology abounds in our schools today—productivity software, instructional software, and informational software. There is no doubt that our teachers need training in the use of all this technology to be able to use it to teach our children the most effectively. It is the responsibility of the library media specialist to provide inservice training to teachers in the area of information technology so that they can make effective use of information in electronic formats, including electronic databases and the Internet.

At the most basic level, teachers should be able to use the library's online public access catalog effectively. The library media specialist may need to offer brief inservice training for access and searching techniques. Some of the online public access catalogs allow users not only to search by author, title, subject, and keyword, but also to put selected titles in a bookbag-type feature. Teachers using this feature can build booklists and bibliographies from the comfort of their classrooms or, if the catalog is available on the Web, from their homes.

Training in the use of Boolean operators (AND, OR, or NOT) is a must, since Boolean logic is applicable in all electronic settings—online catalogs, encyclopedias, periodicals databases, and the Web. Quite a few of our teachers have been in the classroom for many years and may not be as technologically savvy as they would like to be. The library media specialist may provide instruction in Boolean logic through demonstrations, handouts, or the use of some of the excellent tutorials available on the Internet, such as *Boolean Searching on the Internet: A Primer in Boolean Logic* from the University at Albany Libraries at <http://library.albany.edu/internet/boolean.html>.

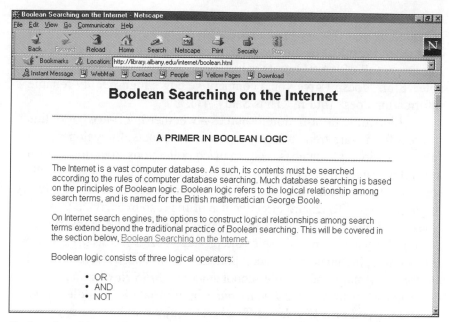

Boolean Searching on the Internet: A Primer in Boolean Logic from the University at Albany Libraries, reprinted with permission from Laura B. Cohen.

Productive, efficient Web searching is an area in which our teachers frequently need instruction. The library media specialist may offer a workshop on effective use of major search tools. Teachers may not be aware of the differences among search tools: search engines, such as Google; subject directories, such as Yahoo!; and metasearch tools, such as ProFusion. Using identical search terms, the library media specialist can demonstrate each type of search tool and results achieved with each. For teachers working with elementary age students, the library media specialist can provide training in using *AskJeeves for Kids* at <http://www.ajkids.com>, *KidsClick* at <http://kidsclick.org>, and *Yahooligans* at <http://www.yahooligans.com>. When your library media specialist trains your teachers, your teachers are then more effective technology instructors for your students.

Beyond good search techniques, the library media specialist should teach teachers how to evaluate what they find on the Internet. Teachers need training to look at Web sites with a critical eye. Common criteria for judging Web sites are content, currency, accuracy, authority, and objectivity. Does the site contain relevant, comprehensive information? Has it been updated recently? Is the information contained therein accurate when compared with information found in a standard, reputable reference work? Who published the site, and what are their credentials? Is the topic presented in an objective, unbiased manner? Teachers need training and guided practice in Web site evaluation. This training can be provided by your library media specialist. As noted by Patricia Schroeder, President of the Association of American Publishers, "The Internet is full of 'stuff' but its value and readability is often questionable. 'Stuff' doesn't give you a competitive edge; high-quality reliable information does" (qtd in "Thus Said": 41).

Electronic information resources—whether in CD-ROM or online Internet form—are tremendously expensive products. Encyclopedias, full-text periodicals databases, specialized collections in various subject areas (biography, literary criticism, historical newspapers, specialized science references) are the types of electronic resources that your library might purchase. To ensure effective use of the resources, once purchased and installed, library media specialists must provide inservice training for teachers in the use of the products. *SIRS Knowledge Source*, for example, includes various components: *SIRS Discoverer*, appropriate for elementary and middle school students; *SIRS Researcher, Government Reporter*, and *Renaissance*, appropriate for middle schoolers and up; and *SKS WebSelect*. Teachers require training to use these resources effectively.

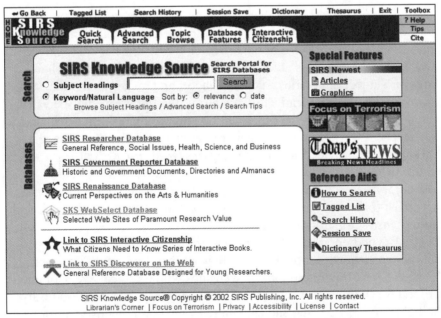

SIRS Knowledge Source, reprinted with permission from SIRS Publishing, Inc.

Teachers also need to know the focus and various features of specialized electronic products (for example, H. W. Wilson's *Biographies Plus, Illustrated;* Gale's *Contemporary Literary Criticism;* ProQuest's *Historical Newspaper Collection*; and McGraw-Hill's *Access Science*, just to name a few) so that they can assist their students in using them the most productively in research. The library media specialist should conduct training sessions on these electronic information products and provide handouts and tip sheets to assist teachers.

When can this inservice training in information technology take place? Often library media specialists will offer Technology Tuesdays or Workshop Wednesdays. A calendar is published for the month, six weeks, or nine weeks, with topics scheduled so that teachers can see what is offered on what upcoming date. The time may be before school (perhaps with coffee and pastries) or after school for an hour or so. Another option would be opening-of-school inservice days, in which teachers rotate through sessions or similar inservice days during the school year. Many teachers have acknowledged the need and usefulness of this training. Their comments: "We have all this information in place. We need to know how to use it so that we can use it with our children. What productive inservice sessions these would be." Expensive, licensed databases will be more effectively utilized if teachers (1) know they exist, (2) receive training in their usage, and (3) subsequently feel comfortable using them in instructional settings.

READING

Library media specialists are traditionally expected to contribute to the school program in this area because, historically, libraries have been known for collections of books and the promotion of reading. Having a quality collection of appropriate books and matching the right book to the right reader are long accepted duties of the school library media specialist. Reading is a basic skill—a prerequisite skill for success in other school subjects, information literacy, and independent learning and information acquisition in life. Yet with the advent of television, video, video games, and computers—technology—we sometimes forget the importance of reading. We may neglect that portion of school libraries, both with our money and our time.

As funding for libraries has remained at a constant level, or in some cases, even fallen, book budgets have suffered as expenditures for technology needs have mushroomed (Miller and Shontz 50). School libraries require adequate funds for collection development so that both print and nonprint needs can be addressed. Beyond having the books, though, your library media specialist needs to be sure to promote them, to promote reading.

Various events throughout the calendar year lend themselves to reading promotion: Read Across America in March in conjunction with Dr. Seuss's birthday, the American Association of School Librarians' School Library Media Month and the American Library Association's National Library Week in April, ALA sponsored Teen Read Week in October, and Children's Book Week sponsored by the Children's Book Council in November.

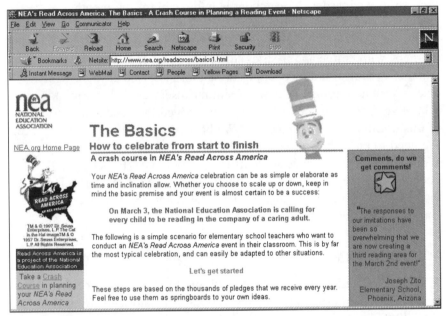

NEA's Read Across America celebration, an annual March event, reprinted with permission from the National Education Association.

Other opportunities to promote reading might focus on authors, on the books themselves, or on book discussions. Once students have discovered an author (whether it be Patricia Polacco or Jan Brett at the elementary level or Richard Peck, Will Hobbs, Lois Duncan, or Walter Dean Myers for the older students), they are fascinated by that author. Displays of the author's works, visits to the author's Web site, or perhaps even a personal appearance by the author at your school work extremely well to promote reading.

Book displays in the library media center or in appropriate display areas throughout the school may focus on an event (the Olympic games), a holiday (Kwanzaa), a month celebration (Women's History Month), or a topic currently of great interest in your school (patriotism and service to country). Book talks that feature works on a certain theme (young adults' struggle to grow and develop self) or recent award winners (the last 10 Newbery Award-winning books) will focus students' attention on books they might otherwise miss.

Many library media specialists are now sponsoring book clubs or literature circles for students. "Bagels and Books" or "Brown Bag It with a Book" allow for breakfast or lunch discussions of works selected and read by all members of the group. Literature circles, facilitated by the library media specialist, allow students to select and discuss novels and develop a real passion for books and literature.

PROGRAM ADMINISTRATION

Given all these elements, it is critical that your library media specialist be a strong administrator for your school's library media program. Dr. David Loertscher, Professor of Library and Information Science at San José State University, proposes that an effective library media program includes collaboration, information literacy, information technology, and reading (Loertscher, *Reinvent* 6). He asserts that the library media specialist who leads this quality library program must have vision and energy. Vision and energy are necessary qualities for today's library media specialist as he manages and implements his program within the whole school context.

Information Power: Building Partnerships for Learning states, "The library media specialist is an advocate for the library media program and provides the knowledge, vision, and leadership to steer it creatively and energetically in the twenty-first century" (5). Your library media specialist should have a vision for his program and a strategic plan. He should have goals and objectives for the program that dovetail into the mission, goals, and objectives of your school. He should be a member of the school improvement team, the principal's advisory committee, or whatever this key group is called within your school. Through participation on this team or committee, the library media specialist is able to connect the library media program to the larger school picture and communicate its potential to key teachers in the school.

As a program administrator, the library media specialist is responsible for budgeting, staff, facilities, scheduling, policies, and procedures. He must use the funding available to him to develop a collection that meets the instructional and general interest needs of the school. He must, in many cases, manage and supervise support staff—clerical workers, parent volunteers, and student helpers. He is in charge of and responsible for the library facility in which he works, and he develops policies and procedures that promote flexible and equitable access to library resources. Beyond effective administration within, your library media specialist should work to connect your school library to the larger learning community. He should participate in formal or informal conversations and cooperative ventures with local public libraries as well as college and university libraries.

What else should you expect from your library media specialist in the area of program administration? Your library media specialist should be knowledgeable in the area of copyright and should promote compliance with federal copyright law in both print and nonprint formats within your school. Beyond copies at the copy machine and proper use of video for instruction, your library media specialist should raise teachers' and students' awareness of the current copyright issues in our digital environment. Most material on the Internet is copyrighted. Use of information from the Internet (as with use of information from traditional resources) is subject to the Fair Use guidelines. Your library media specialist should explain the concept of intellectual property and encourage your faculty and students to practice ethical behavior in their use of information.

A library media specialist with a vision for the 21st century will recognize the need to provide access to information for students in a variety of ways. He will recognize that students need and look for information from locations other than the library itself—from the classroom,

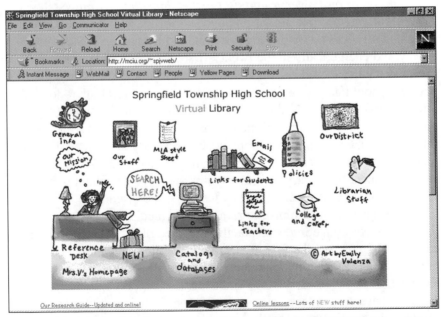

Springfield Township High School Virtual Library Web page, reprinted with permission from Joyce Kasman Valenza.

from home. He will realize the importance of providing virtual reference services, perhaps 24/7, and will have developed a Web page for the school library media center, such as the one on page 28 developed by Joyce Valenza for Springfield Township High School Library.

Items on this Web page may include the school library's online catalog; pathfinders—subject-oriented documents that guide students to quality print and online resources for a particular project or assignment; links to electronic databases; links to quality Web sites, perhaps organized by subject area; and other links that the library media specialist feels are informative and necessary. The library media specialist might have a virtual style sheet section on the Web page with links to sites that explain how to cite sources using APA or MLA style. He might also have a section of links for teachers—a virtual professional collection.

Your library media specialist is called upon to be an effective and efficient administrator of the library media program. He is called upon to administer a program that is in sync with and meets the needs of the school.

LEADERSHIP

You should expect your library media specialist to take a visible leadership role within your school. The library media specialist is, in almost every state, a teacher with additional licensure or with an advanced degree in library science (Perritt 50). This person is an educational specialist, tooled and ready to be an instructional leader within your school. When you consider it, your library media specialist has a unique perspective of the school culture and climate: he works with every grade level, every teacher, and every student. His view of the school is cross-curricular and cross-grade. He sees a child come in as a kindergartner and graduate as a fifth grader. He sees the scope and sequence of curriculum, content, and instruction because he works with all teachers and all students. He is a natural member of curriculum development teams and school improvement teams.

You should also expect your library media specialist to take a visible leadership role outside your school by raising the awareness of parents and the larger learning community concerning the strengths and benefits of a quality library media program. Parent-teacher associations provide great potential for additional funding for library resources and rich pools of library volunteer possibilities—but only if the library program is visible to the parents. It is the library media specialist's job to take a leadership role—to share with parents the mission and goals of the library media program and to offer examples of opportunities for parents to contribute to the achievement of these goals.

It is also the library media specialist's responsibility to be sure that the larger learning community is aware of the activities and benefits of a strong school library media program—through newspaper articles, guest appearances at local civic clubs, and open houses in which community and business leaders are invited to visit to discover what today's school library media program is all about.

AND IN RETURN . . .

What does your library media specialist expect from you, the administrator of the school? First, your library media specialist expects and needs adequate resources—an adequate budget to develop a collection to meet the instructional and general interest needs of the school population. Second, he expects and needs adequate staff. Depending upon the student enrollment in your school and the level of library usage by the students and teachers, your library media specialist needs assistance—clerical assistance and, perhaps, additional professional staff.

Third, your library media specialist needs no outside duties, such as lunch, hall, or bus duty, during the contract day. Before school and after school, during lunch, and during class changes—these are times that the library media center should be available to students and teachers.

Fourth, and critical, your library media specialist needs time in his schedule to meet, plan, and collaborate with classroom teachers. It is through these collaborative planning opportunities that the library media specialist is able to connect library activities to classroom content and integrate information literacy skills instruction.

Finally, your library media specialist needs your support in the effort he is making to develop a dynamic, effective, student-centered library media program. Does principal support make a difference? Dr. Gary Hartzell, Professor of Educational Administration at the University of Omaha, Nebraska, speaking at the June 4, 2002, White House Conference on School Libraries, shared the following thoughts:

> I worked for three years as a consultant in the National
> Library Power Program, funded by the DeWitt Wallace
> Foundation. I saw a lot of innovative and powerful
> library programs all over the country, in small towns
> and big cities, and one of the common elements in
> every one of them was a dynamic librarian. The other
> common element in all those programs was a commit-
> ted principal—no program was successful without one.
> We have enough research on the principal's role to

know that the principal is a key player, perhaps the key player, in library media programs that make a difference. Just review for a minute what you heard earlier. Library programs that make a difference not only have a certificated librarian in place, an adequate support staff and up-to-date and large collections—all monetary investments—they also have schedules that allow the librarian time to collaborate with other staff members. The librarian serves on curriculum committees, provides measures of staff development, and participates in a wide variety of school operations. None of this happens if the principal doesn't want it to. The research evidence also is clear that teachers collaborate more with other teachers and with the librarian when the principal openly encourages it and makes schedules that facilitate it . . . Opportunity rests in the principal's hands. The principal is an absolutely essential element in maximizing the return on library investment (Laura Bush Foundation 6–7).

RESULTING IN . . .

If you see all these elements visible in your library media program— if you note that your library media specialist is involved in such activities as we have discussed—and if you are willing to provide the support listed above in return, your library media program can be an integral part of the instructional program of your school. Your library media specialist can be a valued instructional partner on your instructional team. As library media specialists

- collaborate with classroom teachers,
- teach students information literacy skills,
- instruct teachers in the effective use of information technology,
- promote reading,
- administer the various essential program components, and
- display leadership within your school,

they actively contribute to student achievement, helping students become information literate, independent, lifelong learners. Test scores rise.

Understanding that a strong library media program positively impacts student achievement, some of the things that I, as an administrator, can do to support this program within my school are as follows:

❑ Meet with my library media specialist to discuss how the library media program fits into the instructional program of the school

❑ Provide adequate staffing for the library

❑ Provide funding for library resources

❑ Support reading promotions sponsored by the library

❑ Foster a culture of collaboration within my school

❑ Support the library media specialist as he works to meet and cooperatively plan with classroom teachers

❑ Support the integration of information literacy skills instruction into the content area curriculum

❑ Encourage (perhaps even require) classroom teachers to collaborate with the library media specialist on appropriate units of instruction

❑ Utilize the library media specialist's expertise in the area of information technology, by giving him the opportunity to

    ❑ work with the teachers to understand the differences between Web sites and licensed paid databases

    ❑ train teachers in effective search strategies for the Internet

    ❑ train teachers in the evaluation of Internet resources

    ❑ train teachers in the use of licensed paid databases

❑ Expect and support ethical use of information within my school

❑ Support my library media specialist's efforts to provide access to information resources beyond library walls

❑ Recognize my library media specialist as a teacher, an instructional partner, an information specialist, and a program administrator

❑ Request that my library media specialist serve on key committees for the school—curriculum, technology, and school improvement, for example

❑ Give my library media specialist the opportunity to explain the library's mission and goals to key parent and community groups

❑ Support my library media specialist in his attempts to connect with the larger learning community—public libraries, colleges and universities, and museums, for example

3

What Teachers Should Know and Expect:
The Library Media Specialist as a Teacher

D o you know what your librarian's role is in your school? How does he fit into the grand scheme of things? Is he merely a keeper of books and other instructional materials, or does he have other, more critical roles to play? Test your knowledge by taking the pretest below.

TEACHERS' PRETEST

Respond to each of the following statements by answering true *or* false.

My librarian

1. is concerned and knowledgeable about the curriculum of our school.
2. adds to the collection resources that support the school's curriculum.
3. suggests instructional resources for me to use in my classroom.
4. promotes reading.
5. has standards of his own to teach students.
6. is an instructional colleague/a teaching partner for me.
7. reinforces what I teach in the classroom in the library.
8. teaches my students how to access, evaluate, and use information.
9. helps my students learn how to use information ethically.
10. makes a difference in the academic achievement of my students.

Did you answer *true* to each of these statements? If so, you are a teacher in a school that has a strong librarian and a strong library media program. If you were not able to answer affirmatively to all of them, did any of them surprise you? All of these are things your librarian can and should be doing.

YOUR LIBRARY MEDIA SPECIALIST AS A TEACHER

In 1998, the American Association of School Librarians and the Association for Educational Communications and Technology published the newest set of guidelines for school library media programs, *Information Power: Building Partnerships for Learning*. Critical here is the subtitle of this work: *Building Partnerships for Learning*. With this publication, library media specialists were identified as partners in teaching for learning. Students and student achievement are at the center of everything that library media specialists do. Numerous studies, as related in Chapter 1, have shown that where library media programs are strong and where library media specialists take an active role in the instructional program of the school, academic achievement is higher.

We live in an information age, but in the K–12 environment, we also live in a standards-based, high-stakes testing age. We want our students to be independent, lifelong learners, but we also want them to perform well on standards-based tests. How do we achieve both? Where do these two goals meet? Where does it all come together? It comes together in the library media center with library media specialists collaboratively partnering with teachers in relevant, authentic instruction. So, you want to raise your students' test scores? Let's take a look at how this can be accomplished.

In your school, library media specialists fulfill many roles. In addition to administering their programs (staff, facility, budget, and so on), library media specialists are teachers, instructional partners, and information specialists. It may be foreign for you to think of your library media specialist as a teacher, yet most states require that school librarians first be certified teachers (Perritt 50). As noted earlier, in Canada, library media specialists are even called *teacher librarians*. What can you expect your library media specialist to teach your students? Library media specialists focus more on skills, resources, and process, whereas you teach content.

The Research Process

It is common practice in schools to teach students a writing process, to encourage or even to require writing across the curriculum, and to have a district-adopted writing plan. It is much less common to teach a research process. We teach students to brainstorm, prewrite, write a rough draft, edit, and revise, but we don't typically teach them that research is a process with clearly defined steps that should be followed. We encourage writing across the curriculum; in fact, in many states, standards require it. Required, consistent, structured research across the curriculum is more of a rarity. Many school districts have adopted a K–12 writing plan, with specific skills to be mastered at each grade level. It is much less common to have a district-adopted research process model. Yet we all expect students to "do research," to have information search skills, and these are skills that they will need in life. Your library media specialist can assist you in teaching the research process to your students.

Carol Collier Kuhlthau has done extensive research into the stages of the research or information-seeking process. Actions, thoughts, and feelings are universal as students work through an information-seeking problem (Kuhlthau 41–42). There are numerous process models available that students can use to help them structure and order their research or information-seeking.

One process model, useful particularly for elementary school students, is AASL's KidsConnect Model. The KC Research Toolbox for Students sets forth four basic stages, or phases, of the research process: "I Wonder," in which the student thinks about and asks a question;

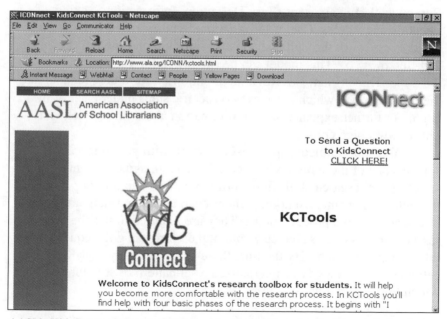

AASL's KidsConnect's Research Toolbox for Students, reprinted with permission from the American Library Association.

"I Find," in which the student locates the information he or she needs; "I Evaluate," in which the students tries to judge and understand the information he or she has found; and "I Share," in which the student develops a product of some sort to share the information he or she has learned. For further explanation and information about this model, visit *KCTools* at <http://www.ala.org/ICONN/kctools.html>.

Another popular research process model is Flip It, developed by New Jersey middle school librarian, Alice Yucht. The Flip It model requires students to Focus (on the research topic), Link/Locate (link to prior knowledge and locate resources), Input/Interpret/Implement (gather, interpret, and use information), and produce a Payoff/Presentation (put it all together for a final product) for Intelligent Thinking (Yucht 89). For further explanation and information about this model, visit <http://www.aliceinfo.org/FLIPit.html>.

A third popular research model is the Pathways to Knowledge framework, developed by Marjorie Pappas and Ann Teppe. This particular model emphasizes that research is a nonlinear process and assists students with suggested resources and strategies as they move through the Appreciation, Presearch, Search, Interpretation, Communication, and Evaluation stages. For further explanation and information about this model, visit <http://www.pathwaystoknowledge.com/the-model/graphic>.

Yet another popular research model is the Big 6, an information problem-solving model developed by Mike Eisenberg and Bob Berkowitz. Using six steps (Task Definition, Information Seeking, Location and Access, Use of Information, Synthesis, and Evaluation), students can work through and solve an information problem (Eisenberg and Berkowitz 5). This model can be simplified for younger students to the Super Three (Plan, Do, Review) or amplified for older students into the Little Twelve, which outlines two specific steps under each of the Big6. For further explanation and information about this model, visit <http://www.big6.com>.

Your library media specialist can work with you to teach your students one of these research process models. Imagine students who start to learn research skills in the primary grades and build upon them throughout elementary school, perhaps even utilizing a standard school or district-adopted process model. They are required to use the same research process across the curriculum, therefore using it frequently and internalizing the steps. By the time these students finish their K–12 educational careers, they have internalized a set pattern or structure within which to "do research."

Search Skills and Search Strategies

If we are going to require students to do research, or to seek information, we need to equip them with search skills and strategies. Your library media specialist can teach your students these skills. At a very early age, students need to differentiate between subject and keyword searches. This awareness is critical, even to online catalog usage.

A student searching for books about dogs will get very different results in terms of return rate and relevance using a subject search and a keyword search. When the student does a subject search for dogs, he or she might retrieve 12 items, which means 12 works have been cataloged under the subject heading *Dogs* and therefore contain a good bit of information about dogs. On the other hand, when a student does a keyword search for dogs, the result may be 244—2,440 occurrences of the word *dog* somewhere in the records in the online catalog. Students who do not have a clear understanding of this concept can quickly become frustrated: "Why did this come up when it is not really a book about my subject?"

Another critical concept that your library media specialist can convey to searchers is the difference between controlled vocabulary and synonyms. No, there are no entries in the online catalog for "Cars." This does not mean that the library has no books about cars. The appropriate, acceptable term within the controlled vocabulary of acceptable subject headings for moving vehicles of this type is *Automobiles*. Granted, in this case, the student searching for works about cars should find a cross-reference in the catalog that refers him to the proper term, *Automobiles*. However, the student still needs to understand that library materials are organized using pre-determined, acceptable terms. Comprehension of this concept will save many students much frustration.

When searching on the World Wide Web, the student may need to brainstorm and think creatively. If he or she is looking for information about cyclones and finds little, perhaps he or she should also search under tornadoes and twisters. This need to think of and use synonyms especially comes into play when students use the Internet, which has no controlled vocabulary of acceptable subject headings.

Effective Internet Use

In this Internet age of information explosion, students need help in using the Internet efficiently and effectively. Your library media specialist can assist students in many ways. First, the library media specialist can suggest appropriate search tools. Younger children can be steered to *Yahooligans* <http://www.yahooligans.com>, *Ask Jeeves for Kids* <http://www.ajkids.com>, or *KidsClick!* <http://kidsclick.org>.

Next, he can teach your students how to effectively use search tools. Subject directories lend themselves to working down, through the hierarchy, from broad to narrower topics. Search engines lend themselves to searches for specific terms. Some search tools allow a natural language search, such as "Why is the sky blue?" or "How do spiders spin their webs?" while others search keywords, such as "sky color" or "spider web."

Older students may be ready to learn the difference between simple searches and advanced searches, as well as unique features of the various search tools. Many of the search tools, such as Altavista and Google, allow the user to search specifically for images or for audio or video files. Second generation search tools, such as Google and WiseNut, rank sites retrieved according to relevance of terms searched, rather than merely the number of times search terms appear. Your library media specialist can share these usage tips with your students, greatly improving the effectiveness and efficiency of their searches.

Your library media specialist can also teach students the concept of Boolean logic, searching using the operators *AND, OR,* and *NOT.* Boolean logic, named for the English mathematician George Boole, can be compared to the union and intersection of sets in math. Using the operator *OR* is comparable to the union of sets. It broadens a search, pulling up results that contain any of the specified terms. For example, entering the words *teenager OR adolescent* will pull up results that have either term present.

Using the operator *AND* is comparable to the intersection of sets. It narrows a search, pulling up only results that contain both terms. Entering *crime AND poverty* as the search term will pull up only results that have both terms present. Similarly, the operator *NOT* narrows a search, eliminating results that contain the specified term. A student doing research on a tiger might do well to limit or narrow his or her search by using *tiger NOT woods* as the search term.

Once your students understand the use of these Boolean operators, they are better able to construct focused searches that retrieve quality results. (Boolean operators are used in online catalogs, in periodicals databases, and in Internet search tools. When using Internet search tools, choosing the advanced search will typically give students the opportunity to use Boolean logic. Sometimes the operators appear as clickable choices in pull-down menus.) Look to your library media specialist to teach your students how to perform effective searches on the Internet using appropriate search tools.

Web Site Evaluation

If students are to use the vast electronic storehouse of information and data known as the Internet, they certainly must be taught to evaluate what they find. On the Internet we find good information, bad information, inaccurate information, biased information, and useless information. Evaluation is the highest level thinking skill on Bloom's taxonomy, and we are asking/expecting/requiring students to evaluate what they find on the Internet. This is not intuitive for our students. Your library media specialist can teach them how to evaluate what they retrieve.

Numerous checklists and guides exist for evaluating Web information. A simple set of evaluation questions, as suggested by Nancy Polette, Lindenwood University professor, author, and workshop presenter, in her "Research Without Copying" workshop, might be "Who put it up?" "Why did they put it up?" and "What do they want you to do with it?" A more comprehensive, yet not terribly involved, evaluation could use the following criteria:

- Content—Does the site have the information that you need?

- Accuracy—Does the information found on the site agree with information on the same topic found in a reputable, published, edited reference source?

- Authority—Who put up the information, and what credentials do they have?

- Objectivity—Is the information presented in an unbiased, objective way?

- Currency— How recently was the site published or updated?

It is critically important that students learn to evaluate information that they locate on the Internet. Your library media specialist is qualified to teach your students these evaluation skills.

Use of Databases

Of course, high quality information is available for students to use for information research purposes in subscription databases. Some that you might find in your school are as follows:

- SIRS *Discoverer* and SIRS *Knowledge Source*

- *BigChalk Library* and *BigChalk Library Elementary*

- *EBSCOhost* and *EBSCO Searchasaurus*

- Gale *InfoTrac Student*, *InfoTrac Junior*, and *InfoTrac Kids*

- *Proquest Platinum, JuniorQuest*, and *KidQuest*

- H. W. Wilson's *Readers Guide for Young People*

These databases include many full-text periodical articles. Some also include basic encyclopedias, standard reference works, and current news events. Your library media specialist will tell you which products your school subscribes to. Many states now even provide access to subscription databases as virtual reference libraries for students:

- Alabama Virtual Library at <http://www.avl.lib.al.us/>

- Connecticut's Digital Library at <http://www.iconn.org>

- Kentucky Virtual Library at <http://www.kyvl.org/html/k12/k12.shtml>

- North Carolina's NCWiseOwl at <http://www.ncwiseowl.org/>

- Tennessee's Electronic Library at <http://www.state.tn.us/sos/statelib/tel/>

Several teaching challenges exist here. First of all, the library media specialist must teach students that although they may use the Internet to access the information contained in online databases, it is not

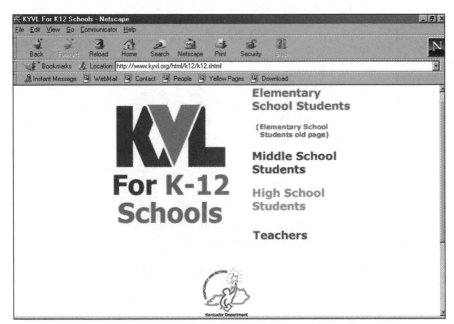

Kentucky Virtual Library for K–12 Students, reprinted with permission from the Kentucky Virtual Library.

part of the World Wide Web. While the Internet is a vast database of unchecked, unedited information, online subscription databases are composed of quality information that has been checked and edited. Second, the library media specialist must expose students to the various subscription databases available for use. Search skills and strategies are somewhat universal, but each database has its own special features and its own idiosyncrasies. Finally, the library media specialist must teach students to differentiate in database usage. Full-text periodical articles may be found in *ProQuest Platinum* or *EBSCOhost*. Biographical information may be found in H. W. Wilson's *Biographies Plus, Illustrated* or Gale's *Biography Resource Center.* Scientific information can be found in Grolier's *New Book of Popular Science* or McGraw-Hill's *AccessScience*. Students must learn to analyze their information need and then select appropriate sources that might answer that need. Where in the past this skill involved selecting the right reference books, it now also includes selecting the most useful, appropriate electronic resources.

Working with Information (Narrowing, Note Taking, Paraphrasing)

Teachers and library media specialists alike bemoan students' broad choice of research topics and lack of note taking and paraphrasing skills, all the while encouraging them to "put it in their own words." Working with information—processing it—is not intuitive, either. Your library media specialist can assist you in teaching your students these skills. Prior to research, students might do some pre-reading in the library on their broad topic, getting ideas for more narrow topics. They can also use print indexes or database subject trees to narrow their broad topic into a more specific one.

A key to improving students' note taking skills is to get them to come up with questions to focus their research. As they read for information, they write something down/take notes only if the information found answers a question. Note taking can also be improved through the use of graphic organizers. Paraphrasing, another key skill, is one that your library media specialist can assist you in teaching. He can encourage students to read a passage, close the book, and write down key thoughts or summary information in their own words.

Citation of Sources

Students need to begin to learn at an early age to give credit where credit is due. Your library media specialist can assist you in teaching your students not only that citing sources is important but also how to correctly cite these sources. Should you expect fifth graders to cite in MLA or APA format? No, but they should be working on building that knowledge and skill. Kathy Schrock gives excellent suggestions and examples for how first through sixth graders should cite sources in the *Reference & Librarians* section of her Web site, <http://school.discovery.com/schrockguide/referenc.html>. Your library media specialist can assist your students, too, by providing a style sheet specific to resources and databases found in your library. Citing a journal article is not too difficult, but how do you cite a journal article that you retrieved from a subscription database?

SAMPLE CITATIONS

*Our fifth grader is citing her article about the octopus from *Ranger Rick*. Using the pattern for fifth grade suggested by Kathy Schrock, her citation looks like this if she used the print magazine itself:

Schleichert, Elizabeth. "Eight-Armed and Awesome!" <u>Ranger Rick</u> February 2000: 2–9.

If she located her article in the *SIRS Discoverer* online database, her citation might look like this:

Schleichert, Elizabeth. "Eight-Armed and Awesome!" <u>Ranger Rick</u> Feb. 2000: 2–9. <u>SIRS Discoverer</u>. SIRS Discoverer on the Web. Jones Elementary School Library, New York, NY. 15 March 2002 <http://www.sirs.com>.

*Our eleventh grader working on the Berlin Wall finds a relevant article in *U.S News & World Report*. If the student used the print version, the citation, completed in MLA format, is as follows:

Barone, Michael. "1983: Falling Walls, Rising Dreams." <u>U.S. News & World Report</u> (25 October 1993): 58–67.

If the student located the article in the *SIRS Researcher* online database, the citation, in MLA format, might look like this:

Barone, Michael. "1983: Falling Walls, Rising Dreams." <u>U.S. News & World Report</u> 25 Oct. 1993: 58+. <u>SIRS Researcher</u>. SIRS Knowledge Source. Smith High School Library, Chicago, IL. 17 Oct. 2002 <http://www.sirs.com>.

Your library media specialist can teach your students how to do this and provide examples, specific to your library, for them to use as patterns.

Information Literacy Standards

Standards pervade our current educational environment. From Curriculum Frameworks in Massachusetts, to Standards of Learning (SOL) in Virginia, to Texas Essential Knowledge and Skills (TEKS) in Texas, to Academic Content Standards in California, if you teach in a public K–12 school district, you deal with content area standards. What may surprise you is that your library media specialist also has standards

---

THE NINE INFORMATION LITERACY STANDARDS FOR STUDENT LEARNING

Information Literacy

Standard 1: The student who is information literate accesses information efficiently and effectively.

Standard 2: The student who is information literate evaluates information critically and competently.

Standard 3: The student who is information literate uses information accurately and creatively.

Independent Learning

Standard 4: The student who is an independent learner is information literate and pursues information related to personal interests.

Standard 5: The student who is an independent learner is information literate and appreciates literature and other creative expressions of information.

Standard 6: The student who is an independent learner is information literate and strives for excellence in information seeking and knowledge generation.

Social Responsibility

Standard 7: The student who contributes positively to the learning community and to society is information literate and recognizes the importance of information to a democratic society.

Standard 8: The student who contributes positively to the learning community and to society is information literate and practices ethical behavior in regard to information and information technology.

Standard 9: The student who contributes positively to the learning community and to society is information literate and participates effectively in groups to pursue and generate information.

From *Information Power: Building Partnerships for Learning* by the American Association of School Librarians and Association for Educational Communications and Technology. Copyright 1998 by the American Library Association and the Association for Educational Communications and Technology. Reprinted by permission of the American Library Association.

for student learning—nine information literacy standards for student learning, set forth in the 1998 *Information Power: Building Partnerships for Learning*.

As your library media specialist teaches your students, he is working to help them achieve these information literacy standards, skills that will help them to become independent information seekers, capable of lifelong learning. As he teaches your students, he attempts to integrate information literacy skills into the school's curriculum.

He works to help students acquire the skills needed to access information efficiently and effectively, for example, to use the table of contents and index in books correctly or to search effectively on the Internet. He teaches them to evaluate information critically and competently, instructing them to ask, "Does this meet my information need? Is it a good, authoritative resource for me?" He encourages them to use information accurately and creatively, to synthesize the information that they have gathered into a new and unique product.

To ensure that students are independent learners, he helps them to learn how to pursue information related to their own personal interests, perhaps a hobby, a health question, or a future career interest. He helps them to appreciate literature and other creative ways of expressing information by exposing them to the works of new and exciting authors as well as old favorites they may have missed. He encourages them to strive to do their best in information-seeking and knowledge-generation, perhaps providing them with a rubric so that they can self-assess as they gather information.

To assist students in becoming responsible users of information, the library media specialist stresses to them the importance of information in a democratic society, pointing out to them that information is not free, readily accessible, and available in all countries of the world. He emphasizes to them the need to use information ethically at all times, stressing equal access to information, paraphrasing, and citing of information sources. He provides the opportunity for students to develop the ability to perform effectively in a group setting using information, perhaps in a cooperative group research project and presentation of information gathered.

TO TEACH NOT ONLY YOUR STUDENTS BUT ALSO YOU?

What can your library media specialist teach you? The mission of the library media program in today's schools, as set forth in *Information Power: Building Partnerships for Learning*, is to "ensure that students and staff are effective users of ideas and information" (6). Library media specialists are responsible for assisting you in your search for information and ideas. How?

Assistance in Search Strategies

If you want to know the difference among a search engine, a subject directory, and a metasearch tool, your library media specialist is the person to ask. If you want to know which search tool works better for a particular type of search, your library media specialist is the person to ask. If you need assistance using Boolean logic or want to hone your search skills, your library media specialist is ready to assist you.

Effective Use of Instructional and Information Technology

Your library media specialist is ready to assist you by teaching you how to physically connect and operate presentation devices, enabling the entire class to view what you have on screen. He is there to instruct and assist you as you create instructional multimedia presentations. He is there to help you locate the exact ERIC document that you need for your education graduate class.

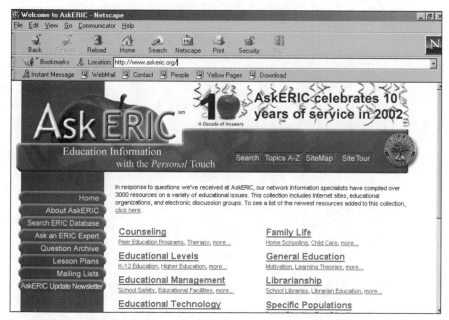

AskERIC is "a personalized Internet-based service providing education information to teachers, librarians, counselors, administrators, parents, and anyone interested in education throughout the United States and the world." Reprinted with permission from the ERIC Clearinghouse on Information and Technology, Syracuse University.

Your library media specialist is there to teach you the finer points of specialized database searching. He is there to teach you how to use the advanced features of your presentation software, such as *PowerPoint*, to work with you on *Kidspiration* or *Inspiration*, and to teach you how to manipulate digital images using a program such as *Adobe Photoshop* or *Microsoft Image Composer*. Your library media specialist is ready and willing to teach not only your students but also you! Think of your library media specialist as a teacher.

4

What Teachers Should Know and Expect:

The Library Media Specialist as an Instructional Partner and an Information Specialist

Your library media specialist wears many hats. In addition to being a teacher, he is also an instructional partner and an information specialist. Let's take a look at how he can assist you in these roles.

YOUR LIBRARY MEDIA SPECIALIST AS AN INSTRUCTIONAL PARTNER

In addition to being a teacher, your library media specialist is available to work with you as an instructional partner—a teaching partner, an instructional colleague, and a fellow educator. If you remember, we noted in the previous chapter that, in most states, library media specialists must first be licensed/certified teachers. Keep this qualification in mind as we take a look at instructional partnerships.

Overview of Students—Across Grades and in a Different Setting

In most situations, a classroom teacher works with a group of students for one year. This is not the case in the library media setting. A library media specialist in a K–5 elementary school has the potential to work with the same students for six years. A library media specialist in a high school, grades 9–12, works with the same students for four years, from immature freshman to senior graduation. This multi-year, cross-grade contact and experience gives the library media specialist a unique perspective of your students.

Also, in a typical library media setting, no grades are given, and there is little, if any, academic pressure. Students usually perceive the library as a friendly, warm, informative, nonthreatening environment. Students may come to use the library in different combinations and peer groups, depending on the schedule for library usage in place. For example, in an elementary school that practices flexible access and flexible scheduling for students, a group of fifth grade students might be in the library completing research while a group of third graders comes to check out books. The library media specialist has the opportunity to observe the fifth graders' interactions with the third grade students. Or, students from three different fifth grade classes might be working together in the library on a common research project, outside of their traditional individual class setting and student group. The library media specialist has the opportunity, once again, to observe these students in this different setting.

If you, as a classroom teacher, need input concerning a student's instructional needs, or if you want to try a new teaching method with a particular group of students or class, consider bouncing your ideas off the library media specialist, a fellow educator and instructional partner.

Promotion of Reading

Another way your library media specialist can assist you as an instructional partner is in the promotion of reading—reading skills and the love of literature. Your library media specialist will, of course, read to your students—exposing them to various genres and to quality literature. From him, they will learn about historical fiction, science fiction, and realistic fiction. They will see and listen to Caldecott winners, from Virginia Lee Burton's *The Little House* (1943) to David Wiesner's *The Three Pigs* (2002), and Newbery winners, from William H. Armstrong's *Sounder* (1970) to Linda Sue Park's *A Single Shard* (2002). Many times, if you communicate what you are studying in the classroom, literary selections can reinforce and complement what you are studying in the classroom.

Your library media specialist might also host book fairs, giving your students the opportunity to purchase books for their own personal libraries. He will promote special reading events in the library, such as Children's Book Week, Teen Read Week, and Read Across America, and he may hold contests that promote reading and reading comprehension, such as Battle of the Books.

Reinforcement, Clarification, and Expansion of Classroom Instruction

In addition to promoting reading, your library media specialist, as an instructional partner, can reinforce, clarify, and expand upon concepts and content that you are teaching in your classroom. If you let your library media specialist know what your students are learning at the present time or in upcoming units of study, he can reinforce your teaching when students visit the library, clarifying and expanding upon concepts taught in the classroom.

An activity in the primary grades, when students are learning to alphabetize by the first letters of words, would be to have students put fiction/easy books in order by the authors' last names. In the middle elementary grades, as students work with estimation skills in mathematics, a fun activity, which also brings in multiplication practice, might be to have students estimate the number of books in the library, working section by section. As an extension, they can use *Excel* to create graphs representative of the collection. Another opportunity for mathematics reinforcement and clarification comes in the area of decimals. Students working on place value can practice the concept using nonfiction books classified using the Dewey decimal system.

The Hundred Divisions

000	**Computers, Internet & systems**		**500**	**Science**
010	Bibliographies		510	Mathematics
020	Library & information science		520	Astronomy
030	Encyclopedias & books of facts		530	Physics
040	[Unassigned]		540	Chemistry
050	Magazines, journals & serials		550	Earth sciences & geology
060	Associations, organizations & museums		560	Fossils & prehistoric life
070	Journalism, publishing & news media		570	Biology & life sciences
080	Quotations		580	Plants (Botany)
090	Manuscripts & rare books		590	Animals (Zoology)
100	**Philosophy**		**600**	**Technology**
110	Metaphysics		610	Medicine
120	Epistemology		620	Engineering
130	Astrology, parapsychology & the occult		630	Agriculture
140	Philosophical schools of thought		640	Home & family management
150	Psychology		650	Management & public relations
160	Logic		660	Chemical engineering
170	Ethics		670	Manufacturing
180	Ancient, medieval & Eastern philosophy		680	Manufacturing specific products
190	Modern western philosophy		690	Building & construction
200	**Religion**		**700**	**Arts**
210	Philosophy & theory of religion		710	Landscaping & area planning
220	The Bible		720	Architecture
230	Christianity & Christian theology		730	Sculpture, ceramics & metalwork
240	Christian practice & observance		740	Drawing & decorative arts
250	Christian pastoral practice & religious orders		750	Painting
			760	Graphic arts
260	Church organization, social work & worship		770	Photography
			780	Music
270	History of Christianity		790	Sports, games & entertainment
280	Christian denominations			
290	Other religions		**800**	**Literature, rhetoric & criticism**
			810	American literature in English
300	**Social sciences, sociology & anthropology**		820	English & Old English literatures
			830	German & related literatures
310	Statistics		840	French & related literatures
320	Political science		850	Italian, Romanian & related literatures
330	Economics		860	Spanish & Portuguese literatures
340	Law		870	Latin & Italic literatures
350	Public administration & military science		880	Classical & modern Greek literatures
360	Social problems & social services		890	Other literatures
370	Education			
380	Commerce, communications & transportation		**900**	**History**
			910	Geography & travel
390	Customs, etiquette & folklore		920	Biography & genealogy
			930	History of the ancient world (to ca. 499 A.D.)
400	**Language**			
410	Linguistics		940	History of Europe (ca. 500 A.D.-)
420	English & Old English Languages		950	History of Asia
430	German & related languages		960	History of Africa
440	French & related languages		970	History of North America
450	Italian, Romanian & related languages		980	History of South America
460	Spanish & Portuguese languages		990	History of other regions
470	Latin & Italic languages			
480	Classical & modern Greek languages			
490	Other languages			

High school biology students studying classification can see real-life application of the concept by looking at the various numbers assigned to books in the various disciplines. For example, works dealing with religion are classified in the 200s, works dealing with pure science are classified in the 500s, works dealing with the arts and recreation are in the 700s, and works dealing with history and geography are in the 900s.

Team Teaching—Planning, Teaching, Evaluating

Library media specialists working as full instructional partners with you will be ready to plan, teach, and evaluate appropriate units with you. Partnerships promote learning. Students benefit from having two or more professional educators instructing them. Three examples of a team-taught unit follow, one for elementary school, one for middle school, and one for high school. In each of these cases, a planning form, such as that found in Appendix B, should be used to organize and document collaboration.

A traditional topic of study in social studies in the elementary grades is the explorers. This topic lends itself well to cross-disciplinary connections and to research. History (who the explorers were, when they explored, what they found), geography (the explorers' countries of origin as well as their discovery locations), math (when they set sail, how long their voyages were, what distances they traveled), and science (under what power they sailed, what weather they encountered) may all be covered within this unit. The library media specialist and the teacher meet to plan the unit, divide teaching and assessment responsibilities, and decide what the student outcomes are to be.

In this case, students might be asked to do any of the following: create a journal that the explorer could have kept on his journey from departure to discovery, justify why an explorer should be named explorer of the year, or write a speech telling how today's world would be different if their explorer had never been born. The teacher will make the assignment and set the criteria for the products with the students. The library media specialist will assist students during the research process, making sure that they follow the steps in the adopted process model. The library media specialist will also assist students in locating the appropriate number of sources (three to five) and variety of sources (encyclopedia, book, Internet) required by the assignment. He will assist students in recording the needed information for citation of sources used. When grading/assessment time comes, the library media specialist will be there with the classroom teacher, assessing not only the products but also the process that the students used to produce those products and the quality of resources used to gather information.

In middle school, a collaborative unit might evolve around the study of ecosystems, communities, and biomes and might include the library media specialist, the science teacher, and the language arts teacher. Initially students will research topics such as food chains and food webs, predators and prey, adaptation of organisms, habitats, population disturbances, and environmental issues. Once they have gathered basic information on these topics and understand the concepts, they can do some study of their local environment and find an issue that interests them. The language arts teacher will then instruct them concerning writing letters to the editor of the local newspaper and making persuasive speeches. Content material, scientific investigation, fact and opinion, persuasive writing and speaking techniques—all are included in this team-taught unit. Educators involved jointly plan, teach, and evaluate the unit.

A collaborative unit at the high school level might involve the library media specialist, English teacher, and United States history teacher. Students interview a person who can describe and relate to them a personal historic event, one that he or she lived through: the Great Depression, World War II, the Civil Rights Movement, the Vietnam War, or the Gulf War. From this interview, students choose a research topic that interests them. The library media specialist assists with research, the English teacher assists with the writing portion of the assignment, and the history teacher focuses on content. The three educators collaboratively plan the unit, using a planning form similar to that in Appendix B, schedule research and instructional time in the library, and assess the students' final products.

In each of these scenarios, at the conclusion of the collaborative unit, teachers and the library media specialist meet to discuss how well the collection met the research needs, how the instruction went, and how they might improve the unit the next time it is taught. The "Teacher/Library Media Specialist Evaluation of a Collaboratively Taught Unit" form found in Appendix B can be used to record this assessment. Students can only gain from having multiple educators. Library media specialists take an active role in curriculum and instruction. Teachers reap the benefits of having a fellow professional partner in instruction.

YOUR LIBRARY MEDIA SPECIALIST AS AN INFORMATION SPECIALIST

A third role that your library media specialist plays, which may best illustrate what you traditionally expect from him, is that of information specialist. In this role, your library media specialist connects you to the information that you need when you need it. He connects you to the professional information that you need to grow as an educator and to the content information that you need to teach your classes.

Professionally: Connect You to Free Online Courses

If you need to brush up on your technology skills or suggest good sites to your students' parents, your library media specialist may refer you to several initiatives sponsored by the American Library Association. *ICONnect* <http://www.ala.org/ICONN/index.html> offers free four-week online courses, delivered via e-mail, on topics such as navigating the World Wide Web effectively and integrating Internet resources into classroom instruction. *FamiliesConnect* <http://www.ala.org/ICONN/familiesconnect.html> lists great family Web sites and suggestions for how to use the Internet safely and effectively in a home setting.

Professionally: Answer Questions About Copyright

You might have questions about copyright:

- How many copies of a periodical article can I make legally?

- Can I make an audio recording of a book for a student who has reading difficulties?

- Can I show this video in my classroom?

- How long can I keep and show this movie that I taped off of regular TV?

- Can I use this image on my Web page?

- Can I copy this workbook page for all students in my class?

- Can I use this image on my bulletin board?

- How much of this popular song can my student use in his *PowerPoint* presentation?

Your library media specialist has the answers to these and other copy-right questions. Copyright refers to the legal, constitutionally guaranteed, exclusive rights belonging to the author of a creative work. While educators enjoy some leeway in using copyrighted works, defined by law as the "Fair Use" guidelines, fair use in no way allows for unlimited use. Your library media specialist can assist you in using copyrighted works legally and ethically to be sure that you are in compliance with federal copyright law.

Professionally: Provide Professional Resources

As an information specialist, your library media specialist can connect you to the professional resources that you need. He will provide access to professional journals, such as *Instructor, Journal of Learning Disabilities, English Journal,* and *Phi Delta Kappan*, both in print and perhaps online through such databases as EBSCO's *Professional Development Collection* or ProQuest's *Professional Education Collection*. If you are interested in participating in an online discussion group or electronic mailing list for your grade and subject area (for example, elementary math, high school English, or teachers of ESL students), he will assist you in locating a quality online discussion group that meets your needs.

Your library media specialist can also suggest resources for you in the area of professional Web sites. He may point you to Kathy

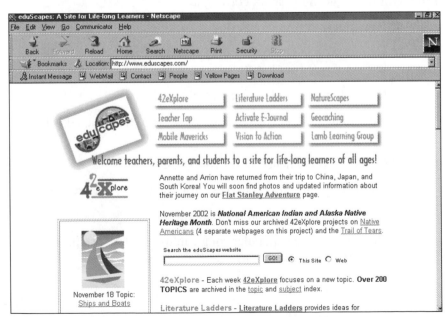

eduScapes: A Site for Lifelong Learners, reprinted with permission from Annette Lamb.

Schrock's *Guide for Educators* at <http://school.discovery.com/schrockguide/>, a fantastic site full of professional and curriculum resources, or he may point you to Annette Lamb's *eduScapes: A Site for Lifelong Learners* at <http://eduscapes.com>, where Dr. Lamb has countless ideas for integrating technology effectively into your teaching.

Your library media specialist might suggest the old standby, *ERIC: Educational Resources Information Center*, at <http://askeric.org>, a collection of more than 3,000 educational resources. If you are interested in WebQuests, he may send you to *Bernie Dodge's WebQuest Page* at <http://webquest.sdsu.edu>. Your library media specialist is an information specialist who can connect you to the professional resources that you need.

Instructionally: Provide Connections to Web Sites

In some cases, you may need specific information for your students. It's history class, and your students are reporting on the presidents. Your library media specialist might suggest that your students start at *POTUS: Presidents of the United States* at <http://www.ipl.org/ref/POTUS/>, or he may suggest resources from the official *White House* site at <http://www.whitehouse.gov/history/presidents/>. He may suggest the *American Memory* site that is available from the Library of Congress at <http://memory.loc.gov>.

In other cases, you might be searching for Web sites that provide the ideas or services that you need. Your students need to do a science fair project. Where should they begin? Your library media specialist may suggest the Science Fair section of the *Internet Public Library* Web site at <http://www.ipl.org/div/kidspace/projectguide/> or *Science Fair Central* at Kathy Schrock's site at <http://school.discovery.com/sciencefaircentral/>. As an information specialist, your library media specialist can connect you and your students to good, quality Web sites.

Instructionally: Provide Connections to Popular Authors

Students as readers and writers themselves are interested in authors as people. Your library media specialist may make a note of authors' birthdays, very popular at the elementary school level, by displaying an author's works during the month or week of his or her birth. He may use other holidays and events during the year to spotlight or highlight an author's works. He might display works by African-American authors, such as Christopher Paul Curtis, Walter Dean Myers, Patricia McKissack, and J. Brian Pinkney, during February, and by women authors, such as Lois Duncan, Mary Downing Hahn, Andrea Davis Pinkney, and Patricia Polacco, during March.

If funds allow, your library media specialist might arrange for an author to visit your school. This is a truly inspiring experience for students. If funds are an issue, your library media specialist might connect students to a particular author electronically via e-mail or through his or her Web site. Two authors who have exceptionally friendly and informative Web sites are Jan Brett, at <http://www.janbrett.com>, and Will Hobbs, at <http://www.willhobbsauthor.com/>.

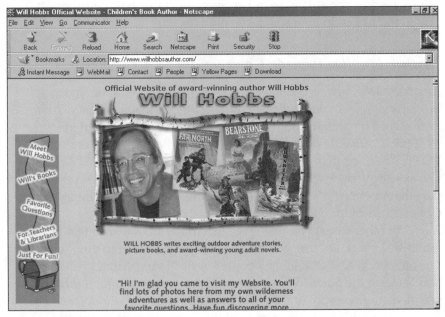

Award-winning author Will Hobbs's Web site, reprinted with permission from Will Hobbs.

Instructionally: Provide Resources to Teach Standards

As an information specialist, your library media specialist can connect you to critically needed instructional resources. As you know, the typical textbook does not contain all the information needed to teach the standards currently in place. You may find yourself required to teach your second graders about ancient Egypt when your social studies textbook does not mention the topic. Another scenario: printed textbooks quickly become outdated. You may find yourself discussing the solar system with your fifth graders, yet your science textbook was copyrighted in 1995. To find additional information to supplement and update the text, consult your library media specialist. He will suggest nonfiction books, such as Ann-Jeanette Campbell's *Amazing Space: A Book of Answers for Kids* (Wiley and Sons, 1997); instructional videos, such as the *Passport to the Solar System* series (Passport to Knowledge); and quality Web sites, such as Bill Arnett's *The Nine Planets: A Multimedia Tour of the Solar System* at <http://seds.lpl.arizona.edu/nineplanets/nineplanets/nineplanets.html> or *NASAKids* at <http://kids.msfc.nasa.gov/>. Your library media specialist is your avenue to resources you need to teach, resources that meet the learning needs of your students.

Instructionally: Build the Collection to Meet Curricular Needs

As an information specialist, your library media specialist is concerned with building a collection of library media materials that will meet the curriculum and instructional needs of your school. He is knowledgeable about the content area curriculum standards in place and tries to select, catalog, and make available materials that reinforce and supplement classroom learning. He tries to purchase materials in various formats (print and nonprint) and on various levels that meet the learning needs of your students.

In addition, he may construct pathfinders to assist your students in locating needed resources both within and outside the library collection. As you assign project or research topics, your library media specialist will structure a path that students can follow to begin to find needed information. The pathfinder may be available in print form in a notebook in the library itself, or it may be available on the Internet through the library's Web page. The pathfinder will suggest subject headings or keywords that students can search in the online catalog to locate resources in the general library collection. It will also suggest reference books, subscription databases, and Web sites that may contain needed information. For sample pathfinders, refer to Appendix C. The library media specialist is an information specialist—for you and for your students.

AND IN RETURN?

The library media specialist serves you and your students as a teacher, an instructional partner, and an information specialist, but what does he expect in return?

First, don't view the library media specialist as a babysitter. Particularly in elementary schools in which the library program operates on a fixed schedule with classes visiting once a week, teachers sometimes tend to view the library media specialist as a "break," a provider of needed planning time. Instead, view your library media specialist as a colleague and teaching partner. Remember that studies have shown that test scores rise when the library media specialist takes an active role in instruction.

Second, request materials for the collection. Your library media specialist values your input and your content area expertise. If you know of a wonderful book or a fantastic video that would greatly enhance the library collection in your subject area, suggest it to your library media specialist for consideration for purchase. If, as you teach and use library resources, you find gaps in the collection or areas in which materials are outdated, again, let your library media specialist know. He will appreciate your interest and willingness to help with collection development in your content area.

Communicate and collaborate with your library media specialist! Keep the lines of communication open and used. Collaborate with this fellow professional educator on appropriate lessons and watch your students benefit.

Finally, recognize the potential that is there. The library media specialist, the library media collection, and the library media program are underused many times by the teachers in a school. See the potential that is there and take advantage of it for your students' sake.

At the June 4, 2002, White House Conference on School Libraries, Faye Pharr, Principal of Lakeside Academy of Math, Science, and Technology, Chattanooga, Tennessee, described her librarian:

Lakeside's librarian once:

- Scheduled classes 30–45 minutes once a week
- Presented authors and read stories once a week
- Checked out books to students once a week
- Taught library skills in January and February
- Gathered materials for teachers—when they asked
- Had some knowledge of the curriculum, but not in detail

She was 'excellent' in doing her own thing. The teachers were 'excellent' doing their own thing. We were wasting precious instruction time until we implemented collaboration.

Today the librarian:

- Plans units of study with grade level teams and individual teachers

- Is involved with the total instructional program

- Now teaches information/library skills as the need arises—usually in small groups

- Reads stories if they directly relate to the curriculum

- Leads kindergarten students through the research process

- Assists students working on computer projects, working in small groups or working independently (2)

Lakeside Academy participated in the Library Power Program, described in Chapter 1, and Ms. Pharr describes the school library now as "empowered." Empower your school library media specialist. Partner with him to make that instructional difference, improving student achievement and raising test scores.

TEACHER SELF-CHECKLIST

Understanding that a strong library media program positively impacts student achievement and that the library media specialist is a fellow educator and instructional partner, some of the things that I, as a teacher, can do to maximize the benefits of the library media program for my students are as follows.

❏ Plan, teach, and evaluate instructional units with the library media specialist

❏ Ask the library media specialist to do the following:

  ❏ work with my students on information literacy skills as an integral part of classroom content instruction

  ❏ suggest a research process model and assist me in structuring my research assignments accordingly

  ❏ provide instruction in usage of the online catalog (beginning in elementary grades with types of searches and advancing to keyword searching, Boolean searching, special features of the online catalog, and access to the catalog from home, if Web-based)

  ❏ suggest the best Internet search tools for my students to use and train them in such usage (age-appropriate search tools, project-appropriate search tools, strategies for advanced/power searching)

  ❏ instruct my students in the critical evaluation of Web sites

  ❏ work with my students to help them distinguish sites on the World Wide Web from licensed, paid databases accessed via the Internet

continued

- ❏ train me and my students on the use of these databases so that we might utilize them more effectively

- ❏ teach my students about the ethical use of information

- ❏ work with my students on how to cite sources, emphasizing to them the importance of giving credit for intellectual work borowed from others

- ❏ Utilize print and nonprint instructional and informational resources available through the library media center

- ❏ Obtain assistance from the library media specialist in the utilization of presentation software and presentation equipment

- ❏ Realize that the library media specialist has a cross-curricular, cross-grade perspective of the students and our school and take advantage of this perspective

- ❏ Work with the library media specialist to promote the joy of reading and appreciation of good literature

- ❏ Work with the library media specialist to help my students connect with authors

- ❏ Realize that the library media specialist can provide connections to various professional resources—journals, Web sites, electronic mailing lists

- ❏ Suggest resources that I feel would enhance the library collection

- ❏ Communicate with the library media specialist, treating him as a collaborative, instructional partner

5

What Parents Should Know and Expect

Your child's library and librarian are not the library and librarian that you may remember from your school days. The books are still there, but today's school library media center contains much more. The library program still involves research, but library-related assignments have gone beyond the report and term paper. The librarian is no longer merely a keeper and dispenser of materials, pulling back issues of magazines from a dusty back room for overnight checkout. He is, rather, a key partner on the instructional team of your child's school. What should you, as a parent, expect from your child's librarian? What is it that he does that can help improve your child's test scores? Read on to find out.

As the research studies discussed in Chapter 1 note, in schools where the library media specialist takes an active role in instruction, student achievement is higher. Reading promotion, information literacy skills instruction, and information technology access are areas that your school library media specialist will address that make a difference in your child's learning.

READING

Most likely, the reading element of the library media program is what you remember from your school days. Libraries have always housed and circulated books—books to be checked out for pleasure reading, for book reports, and for research. Library media specialists still consider books and reading to be a major component of their jobs.

At the elementary level, students are exposed to books, reading, and literature with almost every library visit. In the early grades, library media specialists read aloud stories, folktales, and poetry, reinforcing listening skills and helping students to develop strong comprehension skills. To demonstrate understanding, students may illustrate or dramatize literature that they have heard.

The library media specialist may introduce students to a particular author or illustrator, focusing on that person's works. Young children like to hear the works of Maurice Sendak, such as *Where the Wild Things Are, One Was Johnny, Chicken Soup with Rice,* and *Pierre*, or the works of Chris Van Allsburg, such as *Jumanji, Just a Dream,* and *The Polar Express*. They become familiar with the creator's style of writing and of illustrating. Young children also like to hear new stories about their old character friends, such as Clifford, the big red dog, created by Norman Bridwell; Arthur, the aardvark, created by Marc Brown; David, the naughty little boy, created by David Shannon; and Olivia, the delightful and mischievous little pig, created by Ian Falconer. Library media specialists provide language enrichment and literature appreciation for the early grade students.

As students move to upper elementary grades and middle school, reading is still important. Your child's library media specialist will introduce your child to longer books, in which the material or story is divided into chapters. He will strive to match your child to just the right book, depending on your child's interests. He will help your child to discover whether he or she likes to read historical fiction, adventure stories, sports stories, or animal stories. At this age, your child may have the opportunity to participate in reading book clubs, in which the library media specialist and children select a book to study, such as Louis Sachar's *Holes* or Pam Munoz Ryan's *Esperanza Rising*, and then read and discuss it together in an informal setting, before school, during lunch, or after school.

Library media specialists at the high school level work to promote reading as well. In book displays, they may feature authors such as fantasy writer Terry Brooks, mystery writer Joan Lowry Nixon, historical fiction writer Ann Rinaldi, or realistic fiction writer Jacqueline Woodson, or they may feature certain genres, such as graphic novels, fantasy, or science fiction. Frequently, at the high school level, a reading requirement for a history course will be to read a book set in a particular time period. Nancy Springer's *I Am Morgan Le Fay: A Tale from Camelot*, set in pre-Arthurian England; *Fever 1793* by Laurie Halse Anderson, set in Philadelphia during the outbreak of yellow fever; Mildred D. Taylor's *The Land*, set in the post-Civil War south; and L. M. Elliott's *Under a War-Torn Sky*, set in occupied France during World War II, are examples of books that the library media specialist may recommend.

Psychology and sociology classes might require the reading of novels that portray issues or themes such as child abuse, coping with physical handicaps, or youth violence and crime. In this instance the library media specialist might suggest works such as Margaret Peterson Haddix's *Don't You Dare Read This, Mrs. Dunphrey,* Cynthia Voight's *Izzy, Willy-Nilly*, Terry Trueman's *Stuck in Neutral*, or Walter Dean Myers' *Monster*. Many high school students are ready to advance from young adult novels to adult fiction. Your library media specialist will guide students in this move by suggesting appropriate works such as David Baldacci's *Wish You Well* or some of Mary Higgins Clark's mysteries or Tom Clancy's political novels.

To promote reading at all grade levels, your library media specialist may sponsor programs such as Battle of the Books, in which students read selected works and then compete in a quiz-type setting to answer questions about the books read. He might also promote state reading contests, such as Virginia Young Readers, in which students read books appropriate to their grade level from the list chosen for that year and then vote for their favorite book. Your school might participate in a reading incentive program, such as Advantage Learning Systems' *Accelerated Reader* or Scholastic's *Reading Counts*. These computer-based reading motivation programs provide tests that your child takes after he or she finishes reading a particular book. With satisfactory completion of the test, your child receives a certain number of points for that book. In some schools, competition is strong to be the grade level winner or school winner with the highest number of points. Your school might celebrate Reading Month with special activities or visits from authors or might participate in the National Education Association's Read Across America celebration in honor of Dr. Seuss's birthday, March 2.

Reading, which you remember from your library days, is still a critical component of the school library media program. The program has grown and expanded, however, and now encompasses many other skills and areas.

INFORMATION LITERACY

W hen you were in school and required to do research in the library for your report or term paper, chances are you used books from the reference section and from the general library collection. If the book was in your library, you could count on the information found within it to be authoritative and accurate, at least at the time of the book's publication. Most likely, there were a limited number of sources available for you to use, unless your library participated in an interlibrary loan system with other school or public libraries. In short, your access to information was rather limited. Compare your research experiences to those of your child in today's information-rich world.

Our students today have access to almost limitless information. However, they cannot count on finding information easily and, once they find it, they cannot count on it being authoritative or accurate. The school library media specialist helps them to gain critical information literacy skills. As defined in *Information Power: Building Partnerships for Learning*, the national standards for library media programs, the mission of today's school library media program is "to ensure that students and staff are effective users of ideas and information"(6). To this end, *Information Power: Building Partnerships for Learning* sets forth nine information literacy standards for student learning. (See page 43.) At every opportunity, your library media specialist works to incorporate these standards into learning activities related to what your child is studying in the classroom. When the time comes for research, the teacher and the library media specialist serve as partners in teaching and learning activities and help your child work through the research process.

The library media specialist will help your child develop questions to focus his or her information search. He will assist as your child identifies potential sources of information (books, encyclopedias, magazines, and Web sites), and he will help your child formulate a strategy for using these sources, perhaps first reading information about the topic in a general encyclopedia and then branching out to other sources. Developing skills from using the table of contents and index in traditional reference sources to searching effectively on the Web, the library media specialist will train your child to be able to access information efficiently and effectively (Information Literacy Standard 1).

The library media specialist will also assist your child in judging the quality of information available. All material found on the Internet is not accurate and true, and your child must learn to critically evaluate what he or she finds there. Your child must also be able to match his or her information need with the information source that best fills that need. In some cases, the Internet is the best source. For example, when your child needs current statistical information on a country in Asia, the online *CIA World Fact Book* is one of the best resources available. If your child needs a map showing American and British troop movement for the Battle of Bunker Hill, an American history reference book is probably the best tool. Your library media specialist will help your child learn to evaluate information critically and competently (Information Literacy Standard 2).

As your child works through the information search process, the library media specialist will emphasize the importance of properly using and citing information. He will encourage students to abide strictly by the school's computer acceptable use policy. He will, in cooperation with the content area teacher, teach students to paraphrase as they take notes, to avoid plagiarizing, and to cite all sources properly, giving credit to the creator of the information. He will also make students aware of intellectual property rights and copyright law. What is technologically possible is not always legal or ethical, and the library media specialist cautions students concerning this. For example, if they capture a picture from a Web site to use in their assignment, they need to, at the very least, give credit to the source. The library media specialist will help students to practice ethical behavior in their use of information (Information Literacy Standard 8).

Finally, the library media specialist works with the classroom teacher to help students use information accurately and creatively (Information Literacy Standard 3). Accurate use of information requires that the student accurately report what he or she has found. Creative use of information involves the library media specialist, the teacher, and the student and can determine what sort of final product the student must produce—an oral presentation, a poster, a report, a newsletter, a brochure, or a reflective journal.

As your child works through this research assignment, he or she will most likely follow a research process model that the teacher and library media specialist have chosen. This process model might be the *Big6* <http://www.big6.com>, *Pathways to Knowledge* <http://www.pathwaystoknowledge.com/the-model/graphic>, or *FlipIt* <http://www.aliceinfo.org/FLIPit.htm>, for example. Whatever model your child uses, he or she is following a process to complete the research: he or she follows steps and moves through stages. To use the Big6 as an example, Step 1 is task definition, defining the information problem and identifying what information is needed. Step 2 is information seeking, brainstorming all possible sources of information and then narrowing the list to the best. Step 3 involves location and access, locating information sources, whether they are encyclopedias, magazine articles, or Internet sites, and finding the information within the sources. Step 4 requires the use of information, reading, and taking notes on relevant information. Step 5 is synthesis, which requires organizing and presenting the information, and Step 6 is evaluation, evaluating the information search process used, as well as the final product to be turned in (Eisenberg 1). As your child researches a topic, he or she will move through the stages of this process with the guidance of the library media specialist.

In this technological, information age, your child must be information literate—able to access, evaluate, and use information in an ethical manner. The skills that the library media specialist teaches your child are skills needed to become independent information consumers and producers. As the studies in Chapter 1 relate, when the library media specialist works with the teacher to teach information literacy skills, student achievement increases.

INFORMATION TECHNOLOGY

As noted previously, we live in a technological age. While you, as a student, used the *Readers' Guide to Periodical Literature*, a print index to magazine articles, which gave citations only, your child has access to full-text magazine articles and other reference sources with the click of a mouse. The school library, either on its own, in cooperation with other schools in the district, or as part of a statewide initiative, provides access to electronic subscription databases such as *Gale's InfoTrac*, *Grolier Online*, *SIRS Knowledge Source,* or *World Book Online.* In many cases, licensing agreements allow students to access these databases from home. The library media specialist will train your child in the use of the resources, demonstrating the type of information found within, whether it is encyclopedia articles, magazine articles, or biographical or scientific information. He will teach your child how to search within these databases; print, e-mail, or save the information he or she needs; and properly cite the material he or she used.

To provide easy access to information, the library media specialist may have developed a Web page for the library. Through this Web page, your child may be able to access not only the databases listed above but also the online library catalog and selected, quality Web sites. In addition, he may have developed pathfinders, research and resource guides that your child can use to complete a particular assignment. Appendix C contains a sample pathfinder on Ancient Greece developed for third grade students, as well as a sample high school pathfinder on Africa.

Your child no longer has to "go" to the library to make use of library expertise and resources. Information technology makes library resources available virtually, via computer, throughout the school building and from home.

THE FOUR C'S

The school library media specialist communicates, cooperates, coordinates, and collaborates with your child's teachers. Learning experiences in the library are linked to those in the classroom. Through these learning experiences, your child participates in reading activities, hones information literacy skills, and utilizes information technology.

Expect your school library media specialist to take an active role in what is happening instructionally in your child's school. Expect him to be a "library teacher," as elementary children often say. *Information Power: Building Partnerships for Learning* asserts that "library media programs must be dynamic, enthusiastic, and student-centered" (2). Look for these characteristics in your school's library media program. Is the library a place of buzz and learning activity? It most certainly should be, as your library media specialist helps your child gain critical reading and information skills for life.

AND WHAT FROM YOU?

What can you, as a parent, do to support your child's school library media program?

1. Support and encourage your child's reading efforts. The more a child reads, the better he or she reads. "More recreational reading results in literacy development. There are consistent and positive correlations between the amount of reading children do and their growth in reading" (Krashen 38).

2. Support and encourage your child to properly use information. When your child is working on a research assignment at home, ask if he or she is using a variety of sources and has visited the library's Web page for assistance. Ask your child if he or she is paraphrasing information and crediting sources.

3. Serve as a parent volunteer in the school library media center. Spending time in the library is a wonderful and rewarding way to find out what a school library of the 21st century is really like.

4. Provide support, moral and monetary, for library events, such as Book Fairs.

5. Recognize that the library media program and the library media specialist make a critical and unique contribution to your child's learning and achievement.

If you are a library media specialist reading this chapter, please share this information and these ideas with the parents in your school. Let parents know that you have a copy of this book in your library media center and that a chapter was written just for them. Include information from this chapter in the library newsletter that you send home or in a presentation that you make for the school's parent-teacher organization. Help your parents to become more informed about the key role you play in their children's education.

6

What Library Media Specialists Need to Do

As noted in Chapter 1, numerous research studies have proven the positive impact that a strong library media specialist and a strong library media program have on academic achievement. This chapter contains but a few suggestions—suggestions for action, if you will—for practicing library media specialists who want to make an instructional difference in their schools. What can you as a library media specialist do to enhance student learning? What is it that you do that makes a difference?

COLLABORATION

1. Develop the library media collection so that it is targeted to the instructional program of the school.

    Select and provide resources with curricular needs in mind. Analyze the library collection using either David Loertscher's collection mapping technique or Karen Lowe's resource alignment method. Using these methods will give you quantitative and qualitative data for which areas of the collection are strong and which are weaker. Compare this data to the standards and curriculum. Target the weaker areas for improvement. Solicit requests for materials from content area teachers. Provide a library collection that meets the instructional needs of the school.

2. Know the curriculum—district and state.

    You must know the curriculum in order to build your collection appropriately and to effectively connect with teachers for collaborative instruction. Is classification of plants introduced at the second or the fifth grade level? Depending on the answer, you will need to provide library resources at different reading levels. Is the state planning to add two historical figures to a history standard? You will need age-appropriate biographies about these two people in the library collection. In which grade do students study the explorers? Do you have adequate materials to meet the research needs for that first major research assignment on that topic? You, as the library media specialist, must be thoroughly versed in curriculum.

3. Attend grade level/department meetings.

    You attend these for several reasons. First, you attend grade level/department meetings to reinforce teachers' and administrators' understanding that you are interested in what is happening instructionally in the classroom, that you are an educator, concerned about the instructional program of the school. Second, you attend these meetings to gather information—who is teaching what topic and when? Does a teacher plan to teach a topic differently this year? Will different or additional resources be required? Is there an opportunity for collaboration? Finally, you attend these meetings to give input—input into resources available or lacking and input into instructional strategies and assessments. Your attendance and participation at these meetings goes a long way toward public relations and builds the concept of what today's school library media programs are all about.

4. Serve on standards and curriculum committees.

    As previously noted, you have to be knowledgeable about the standards and curriculum in place in your district and your state. One of the best ways to become knowledgeable and informed is to actively participate on standards and curriculum committees. You will be able to gain valuable information (Is the plan to add an ecology course at the high school or to move civics out of high school and down to middle school?), and you will be able to express the library perspective as it relates to curriculum issues. Your mere presence on the committee is a reminder to other educators of the integral role that the library program should play in instruction.

5. Participate in curriculum development.

    As you become involved with standards and curriculum committees, you might find yourself working to develop curriculum. Jump right in. Have confidence in the knowledge that you have from working with all grades and all content area teachers within the school. You have a unique perspective that can be very useful to other educators and can, in turn, be beneficial to students. Dr. Marilyn Miller, professor emeritus at the University of North Carolina, Greensboro, asserts that the school library media specialist must be perceived as a strong, creative, collaborative professional who is a visible leader in the design of curriculum and instruction appropriate for an information-rich culture" (16).

6. Collaborate with teachers. Meet to plan appropriate lessons cooperatively.

   Collaboration and partnerships, of course, are a dominant theme in *Information Power: Building Partnerships for Learning.* The research studies discussed in Chapter 1 emphasize the positive benefits to student achievement when the library media specialist serves as a collaborative, instructional partner. Realize that you, as the library media specialist, might have to take the lead in this collaborative venture. Teachers might still think of you as the "keeper of the books." You might have to promote your instructional role. Students benefit not only from having more than one instructor but also from observing this collaborative model in action.

7. Team teach and co-evaluate student products with teachers.

   As appropriate, offer to team teach with content area teachers. You may teach the process while the classroom teacher focuses on the content. Your "subject matter" may be selection of appropriate sources for a particular information question or proper citation of the sources used. Your contribution to product evaluation might be to grade those components of the student product.

INFORMATION LITERACY

8. Be vocal for information literacy and work to integrate information-literacy skills instruction into the curriculum.

   If you serve on curriculum committees and participate in curriculum development, use these opportunities to speak up for information literacy and for information-literacy skills instruction as an integral part of content area instruction. Be sure that revised or newly written curriculum includes an information literacy component. Take a look at your school's mission statement. Chances are that it contains a statement concerning "helping students become lifelong learners." The opportunity to talk about information literacy, to point out the importance of those skills, is often there; we must just take advantage of it.

9. Teach information literacy skills to students, as appropriate, as an integral part of content area instruction.

Marcia J. Rodney, principal author of *Make the Connection: Quality School Library Media Programs Impact Academic Achievement in Iowa,* asserts that "with the move to standards-based education, which focuses on what students have learned (proficiencies or outcomes) rather than what is taught (coverage of content), the school library media specialist is in a unique position to help students develop the information literacy skills that will enable them to achieve standards" (3). It is up to you, as library media specialists, to incorporate and integrate information-literacy skills instruction, critical to student achievement, into the content areas. When students become proficient in information literacy skills, they are then able to become competent, independent learners.

10. Be sure that students are able to recognize a need for information and that they have the skills to access, evaluate, and then use the information.

Work to weave information literacy skills into content area instruction. Partner with classroom teachers to give your students the opportunity to learn and practice these skills. Evaluate their competence in these skill areas. Nancy Everhart gives excellent rubrics for assessing students' information literacy skills in *Evaluating the School Library Media Center: Analysis Techniques and Research Practices* (69–78).

11. Explore and examine the various research process models.

Investigate the numerous research process models available, such as Big6, Flip It, I-Search, and Pathways to Knowledge. Read books and periodical articles that explain them. Attend workshops and conferences to learn more about them. Share them with teachers, and use them in your instruction of students. Work for school-wide adoption and consistent use of a particular model.

INFORMATION TECHNOLOGY

12. Work to become informed about the variety of electronic resources available.

If you are in a state that provides a virtual collection for the K–12 environment, first familiarize yourself with that collection. Next, work to supplement it with local purchases. Preview the various database products, periodical and specialized. Become familiar with the features. Look for special ones. Ask yourself: Does this database also include an encyclopedia whereas this one does not? Does this product provide citation examples, specific to the article searched? Does this product also have a professional collection component? Evaluate not only the quality, content, and extent of the database but also the user-friendliness of the interface. The product may have great coverage of resources, including all the major periodicals, full-text, for the past 15 years, but if students are going to have great difficulty using it, even after they have been trained, think twice before you purchase.

13. Train teachers and students to effectively use the licensed databases available.

Do not merely purchase and install the licensed databases, assuming that teachers and students will then discover and use them. Typically this is not the case. Once a database is up and running, publicize it. Send e-mails to faculty. Include sample, content-area-specific usage ideas in your next library newsletter. Offer and provide training sessions to individuals, small groups, and large groups. Structure the training to include not only demonstration but also a hands-on component, if at all possible. If the database is a specialized one, such as Grolier's *New Book of Popular Science Online* or McGraw-Hill's *AccessScience*, for example, make a point to attend the science department meeting to share the word. Teachers and students must be trained to use these licensed database products.

14. Train teachers to effectively use the Internet: to use search tools efficiently and effectively and to evaluate information found.

Usage: If you have teachers on your faculty who still need assistance with Internet searching, plan to offer inservice training or a workshop. Be prepared to demonstrate several of the search tools and discuss the differences among search engines, subject directories, and metasearch tools. Demonstrate the same search on Google, Yahoo! and Profusion to illustrate that different search tools might require different strategies and produce different results. Work with the teachers to understand Boolean logic and to use the advanced or power features of the search tools.

Evaluation: A range of horror stories exist here—everything from the teacher who will not accept an article located in SIRS because it "came from the Internet," to the teacher who accepts, without question, *.com* sites as research citations. Clarify with your teachers the difference between an article accessed in a paid, licensed subscription database and a site found on the World Wide Web, and give them the skills to evaluate the Web sites. Kathy Schrock provides

numerous links to Web evaluation tools from her Web page at
<http://school.discovery.com/schrockguide/eval.html>, even ones
that can be used at the elementary level.

15. Work to provide access to resources at the point of need, even
beyond library walls.

Access to Databases: Support access to licensed databases
from computer labs and classrooms. Yours should be a library
without walls, an information provider at the point of research need.
Students no longer have to "come to the library" to access library
resources and to find good information. The library comes to them.
It becomes "knowledge space" as opposed to an "information
place," providing "connections" instead of merely "collections,"
according to Ross Todd in a keynote paper delivered to the 2001
International Association of School Librarianship Conference in
Auckland, New Zealand.

Virtual Reference Collection: Likewise, construct a Web page
for your library and include a virtual reference collection there,
links to good Web sites that your patrons can use. Consider prepar-
ing pathfinders for various major assignments and posting them to
the Web page to provide guided research assistance, providing scaf-
folding, as Jamie McKenzie discusses (155). Research has always
been a daunting task for our students, but in this information age, it
is particularly challenging. The sheer number of resources can be
overwhelming. Direct students to quality sources so that they can
focus on the information found there.

Connections with the Larger Learning Community: Make
connections with the larger learning community—other area
libraries, businesses, and museums. Contact area public and college
and university libraries. Determine which of their services are available to your students and teachers. Investigate interlibrary loan and
resource-sharing possibilities. Will they loan materials to your
patrons? Is it possible for your senior honors class to make a field
trip to the local university library to use the specialized reference
materials there? Does an area museum offer a traveling classroom
collection of photo or artifact reproductions? Make these resource
connections for your students and teachers.

READING

16. Promote reading for enjoyment. Encourage literature connections to various content areas.

    Do not neglect reading and books, either financially or programmatically, in this information technology age. Keep the reading component in the library. Booktalk to promote good literature. Connect students with authors, virtually if no other means present themselves. Focus on reading during the reading events of the library calendar year. Help teachers connect literary works to the concepts being studied in the classroom: Christopher Paul Curtis's *The Watsons Go to Birmingham* to a study of the Civil Rights Movement, Janell Cannon's *Stellaluna* to the study of animal habitats, or George Levenson's *Pumpkin Circle* to the study of the life cycle of plants, for example. Consider hosting and sponsoring a book club or a literature circle. Encourage your students to participate in state activities such as the Virginia Young Readers Contest or North Carolina's Battle of the Books.

PROGRAM ADMINISTRATION

17. Be familiar with federal copyright law and fair use guidelines.

    You may very well be the copyright expert within your school. Be prepared to answer questions concerning proper and improper, legal and illegal, use of print materials, videos, multimedia, and Internet information. Carol Simpson's latest edition of *Copyright for Schools: A Practical Guide* (2001) lives up to its title. It will give you much information that you need.

18. Promote ethical use of information with teachers and students: appropriate use of the Internet, observance of all copyright laws, proper note taking, and citing of information sources to avoid plagiarism.

    Beyond providing information about copyright and fair use, be sure that you model and promote ethical use of information at all times. Remind students of safe and acceptable use of the Internet. Emphasize that the signed acceptable use agreement signifies respect for guidelines and commitment to abide by policies. Observe copyright laws and fair use guidelines. Model note taking strategies, and set an example by consistently citing information sources.

19. Embrace your roles as teacher, instructional partner, information specialist, and program administrator.

    Information Power: Building Partnerships for Learning calls upon us to practice each of these roles in our school settings. Reread Chapter 1, "The Vision," and strive to teach, to partner, to provide information access, and to administer your library media program.

20. Manage your library media program efficiently and effectively.

    Work to implement policies and procedures and to manage your program—staff, facilities, scheduling, and budget. Collaborate, teach information literacy, promote appropriate use of information technology, and encourage reading.

LEADERSHIP

21. Familiarize yourself with the results of the various research studies that show the impact library media programs have on student achievement.

    Share the results of the studies with your teachers, your principal, your superintendent, your board of education, your community. Implement, in your school, those activities that the studies have shown make a difference. Document what you do that makes an instructional difference.

22. Be an instructional leader within your school.

    Be proactive. Participate in instruction. Use the appropriate brochure for your school level found in Appendix D to discuss the library media program with your principal: *Academic Success @your library: Powerful Partnerships: Your School Librarian and You!* Explain to him or her how full implementation of these principles builds a strong program.

23. Constantly communicate with administrators, teachers, and parents.

    This cannot be emphasized enough. Keep the lines of communication open at all times. Communicate formally through newsletters and memos and informally through conversations and e-mail. Keep your principal informed. Provide statistics concerning library usage, both quantitative and qualitative. Let teachers know about upcoming library activities and initiatives. Solicit suggestions for materials to purchase. When new materials arrive appropriate for their content areas, be sure to let them know. When you attend conferences, share new ideas with them when you return. Remind them of the professional collection available for their use, either in the library or electronically. Be sure that teachers know that you are an instructional partner, there with them to enhance student learning. Communicate this to parents as well. Emphasize, at every possible opportunity, that you are a team player, concerned about student achievement.

24. Be visible and indispensable.

    Gary Hartzell asserts, in *Building Influence for the School Librarian*, that we must work to let those in positions of influence know the important role that we play in the school. Rather than being what Dr. Hartzell refers to as the "invisible school librarian," be visible. Be pleasantly vocal. Be, as Doug Johnson says, the "indispensable librarian."

25. Be an advocate for your library media program and its benefits.

    Speak up for your program with people who matter, who impact your program—parents, teachers, administrators, and boards of education. Provide evidence of the difference that you make instructionally to student learning. Advocacy begins with you!

Are you exhausted? You very well could be. Being a library media specialist is a demanding job. We juggle; we multi-task on a constant basis. Yet we as educators accept this as our job and our responsibility. As instructional personnel in our schools, we are concerned about test scores. Truly, student achievement is the bottom line!

■ American Association of School Librarians. *A Planning Guide for Information Power: Building Partnerships for Learning with School Library Media Program Assessment Rubric for the 21st Century*. Chicago: American Association of School Librarians, American Library Association, 1999. Excellent for its action plan and for the library media program assessment rubric.

■ American Association of School Librarians. *AASL Advocacy Toolkit*. Available at <http://www.ala.org/aasl/advocacy/>. Online access to a *PowerPoint* presentation on advocacy, Talking Points, an *Information Power* brochure, resources guides, and other support materials.

■ American Association of School Librarians. *Information Literacy Standards for Student Learning*. Chicago: American Library Association, 1998. Chapters 1 and 2 from *Information Power: Building Partnerships for Learning*, "The Vision," and "Information Literacy Standards for Student Learning," are reprinted in a separate document for sharing with other educators.

■ Hughes-Hassell, Sandra and Anne Wheelock, eds. *The Information-Powered School*. Chicago: American Library Association, 2001. Gives accounts from Library Power schools and practical ways to implement *Information Power* in your school.

■ Lance, Keith Curry and David V. Loertscher. *Powering Achievement: School Library Media Programs Make a Difference: The Evidence*. San Jose, CA: HiWillow, 2001. *PowerPoint* presentations, scripts, and reproducible handouts detailing results of many of the research studies discussed in Chapter 1.

■ *NASSP Bulletin*. 83:605 (March 1999). Entire issue devoted to information literacy.

■ *Proceedings from the White House Conference on School Libraries*, June 4, 2002. Available from <http://www.imls.gov/pubs/whitehouse0602/whitehouse.htm>. Remarks from First Lady Laura Bush, Faye Pharr, Dr. Gary Hartzell, Dr. Keith Curry Lance, Dr. Susan Neuman, and others.

■ *The School Library . . . Where Learning Meets the Future*. Nassau School Library System, 2000. A 12-minute video "created to bring viewers directly inside what many educators today consider to be the hub of a good school: the library media center"—from container. Available from the American Association of School Librarians.

7

And the Winner Is...

A nd the winner is, of course, the student! For all of us in education, student achievement is the bottom line. Our mission is to
help students become productive citizens who are independent,
lifelong learners. In today's world, student achievement is measured in
great part by test scores. We can improve student achievement by using
staff, resources, and programs already in place in our schools—if only
we know what to look for and what to do with what we find. "The association between library resources and activities and student performance
as measured on state tests has been documented in library and educational research. Research has consistently shown that schools with well-
staffed and well-resourced libraries and with librarians acting effectively
in their role as program administrators, teachers/trainers, and information technology access-providers have higher scores on state tests"
(Smith 23).

HOW MUCH WILL TEST SCORES
RISE?

H ow much will test scores rise? The second Colorado study
reports that "when LM [library media] predictors are maximized
(e.g., staffing, expenditures, information resources and technology), CSAP [Colorado Student Assessment Program] reading scores
tend to run 18 percent higher in fourth grade and 10 to 15 percent higher in seventh" (Lance, Rodney, and Hamilton-Pennell, *How School
Librarians Help Kids* 79). In the Pennsylvania study, the researchers
note that "when all school library predictors are maximized (e.g.,
staffing, library expenditures, information resources and technology, and
information literacy activities of staff), PSSA [Pennsylvania System of

School Assessment] reading scores tend to run 10 to 15 points higher" (Lance, Rodney, and Hamilton-Pennell, *Measuring Up* 59). These represent significant gains in test scores, and they are gains achieved by maximizing the potential of the library media program and the library media specialist.

In this book, we have examined the major research studies documenting the impact of school library media programs on academic achievement and have looked at the key players in the process: the principal, the teachers, and the library media specialist. It is when all the key players have common understandings and expectations and a willingness to work toward this common goal that a collaborative culture evolves: a culture in which the principal understands the potential of the library media program, supports the initiatives of the library media specialist, and expects great things to happen; a culture in which the teachers understand the role of today's library media program in instruction and willingly accept the library media specialist as a full, collaborative, instructional partner; and a culture in which the library media specialist knows the potential that exists and capitalizes on this potential, working with the principal and the teachers to implement the activities that make the difference. A synergy develops. The whole is greater than the sum of the parts. Student achievement is higher.

FROM AN ADMINISTRATOR'S PERSPECTIVE

D r. Mark A. Edwards, Superintendent of Henrico County, Virginia, Public Schools: "Our librarians, now known as library information specialists, will always be purveyors of reading for information as well as pleasure. However, the role of the library and the job of the librarian has changed dramatically in the last few years, evolving the library into a multidimensional, exciting place for a whole menu of educational activities . . . The days of the hushed silence in libraries and the simple checking in and out of books are long past. Our libraries have become centers of learning that provide integral information for every teacher and student in our schools. This change and development is exciting for students and faculty and has opened doors for thousands of students . . . The great menu of tools that we have for information and collaboration will only serve to make learning more fun and more valuable for our students as we move into the 21st century" (4).

Is it fair to expect so much of the library media specialist? C. Rodney Clemmons, principal at Atlee High School, Mechanicsville,

Virginia, and Virginia Educational Media Association's Administrator of the Year, 2001, explains:

> The modern environment has so many opportunities for information access that the passive librarian is soon to be an extinct librarian. It's not enough to build a facility with great resources when patrons can get information over cell phones and PDAs. The crucial difference the librarian has to offer is intelligent assessment of information. In the school setting, the librarian must be an instructional leader who propels the curriculum and access to technology. This can only be accomplished with meaningful support from the principal and a high volume of teacher and student traffic. To accomplish this, the librarian must throw herself and the library in the path of the principal, and she must give kids what they want—good feelings about being in the library and solutions to their problems. The librarian must be both a dreamer and a doer. I expect the librarian to demonstrate 110% commitment to the school's success and to expend double the energy of any other person in the building. The librarian who can't outwork the football coach is just coasting.

Mary Robinson, Principal at Swift Creek Middle School, Midlothian, Virginia, describes the library program's role as follows:

> The library is the center support beam for the entire school. It is 'possible' to teach all of the curriculums without using the library for reinforcement and supplementation, but the curriculums then become very dry and students are simply learning basic facts. Using the library allows educators to teach students how to move to higher levels of thinking and learning. Students learn how to find information and to expand their own learning. Yes, it's possible to run a school without a library, but that school certainly wouldn't be full of the exciting learning opportunities available in a school with a library.

Ms. Robinson's sentiments are echoed by Joyce Price, Principal of Hardin Intermediate School, Duncanville, Texas: "A strong library media program and a media specialist who is an instructional leader will enhance the entire educational process. The support is incredible and is appreciated by every professional in the building."

FROM A TEACHER'S PERSPECTIVE

Teachers who work with strong library media specialists who build quality library media programs appreciate the contribution that the library makes to the instructional program of the school. Bob Jenkins, Spanish 4 and 5 teacher from James River High School, Midlothian, Virginia, states:

> Through the library I have become more technologically literate. The library allows my class to expand beyond the walls of the classroom. There isn't anything I can't find in the library to supplement my educational activities. The librarians have helped me gain more confidence in technology and my confidence level is much higher. I could never have accomplished this by myself. The library is an invaluable resource that everyone should incorporate into their daily plans.

His sentiments are echoed by Angela Jones, sixth grade teacher at Hardin Intermediate School, Duncanville, Texas:

> I am extremely lucky to work with a library media specialist who is dedicated to helping my children understand that there are outside resources available to them that enhance education and make learning fun! I have received countless ideas from Mrs. Cavitt [the library media specialist] and her assistant, Mrs. Harris, that have excited the kids and propelled them to success.

Paul Van De Mortel, social studies teacher at James River High School, Midlothian, Virginia, encourages fellow teachers to fully utilize the library, its staff, its programs, and its services:

> It has been my experience that school libraries are under used. I have found it most expedient to present a topic, and then utilize the talents of our librarians and the vast resources of the library, to enhance the learning process. Students have the opportunity to explore various ways to achieve the objectives of any lesson, that otherwise might be missed by just lecturing about it in the classroom. I have found that students who utilize the library and its resources perform better on their projects and subsequent tests than those who rely solely on the resources of a

classroom. Students also are able to bring fresh, up-to-date information and a new perspective to an ever-changing world. As a teacher of world history, U.S. history, and U.S. government, I have found most of my successes by utilizing the library/media center to its fullest potential.

FROM A LIBRARY MEDIA SPECIALIST'S PERSPECTIVE

Yes, exciting things happen as libraries become central to the instructional program of a school. Julie Van Metre Tate, library media specialist at Atlee High School, Mechanicsville, Virginia, describes growing teacher usage of their library services:

> After teaching Mr. Lumish's world history/geography classes how to create impressive color travel brochures with MS *Publisher*, teachers from other disciplines began requesting the same collaborative service. From mythology to pop culture to biographies, we (the library media specialists) worked with students to research information, locate graphics, and create informational brochures. The same scenario occurred when we taught a physical education class how to create *PowerPoint* presentations on sportsmanship. Immediately, other teachers requested the same assistance, and while teaching the technology, we (the LMS) incorporated both print and nonprint research strategies. The quality of the completed projects indicated a successful venture for all parties involved.

Fran Carleton, library media specialist at Crenshaw Elementary School, Midlothian, Virginia, notes:

> Collaboration is the life's blood of the media specialist! Collaboration moves the library media specialist away from the image of the "keeper of the books" to that of a partner with the classroom teacher. When the library media specialist collaborates or partners with the classroom teacher in teaching Standards of Learning, she and the teacher bring the unit to the students as a team.

Ann M. Martin, library media specialist at James River High School, Midlothian, Virginia, and Winner of the AASL School Library

Media Program of the Year Award for 2002, explains the role of the library in the grand school scheme of things:

> The library serves as the heart of the school, pumping knowledge through all areas of school life. It fuses information with real life experiences. This is accomplished through resource sharing, research instruction, reading opportunities, and cultural connections. The library is a welcoming place where its users explore and discuss intellectual and social issues. A dynamic library program promotes academic achievement and energizes students and staff.

FINAL THOUGHTS

D r. Robert Martin, director of the Institute of Museum and Library Services, reporting on the June 4, 2002, White House Conference on School Libraries, noted the following: "Now we have the research to affirm what [Laura Bush] has long known: good school libraries enhance children's learning. Working together, equipped with the best research and examples of proven school library programs, librarians, teachers, and school leaders can make a difference in student achievement" (Laura Bush Foundation 1).

When administrators, teachers, and library media specialists work together, powerful things happen. Dr. James Baughman states, "The future belongs to those of us who can team and build for the children . . . the group for which we today—here and now—are advocates. The advocacy is for student achievement. School libraries significantly increase student achievement" (18). Do your part. As an administrator, as a teacher, as a parent, as a library media specialist, leverage your library program to maximize student learning and achievement.

Appendix A

Chronological Summary of the Research Studies

Colorado, 1993

Lance, Keith Curry, Lynda Welborn, and Christine Hamilton-Pennell. *The Impact of School Library Media Centers on Academic Achievement.*

Overview:

Researchers from the Library Research Service, Colorado State Library; School Library Media Development, Colorado State Library; and the Colorado Department of Education Resource Center studied data from 221 public schools in Colorado. Elementary, middle/junior high, and senior high schools were studied. Four sets of data for each of the schools were analyzed: U.S. Census data for its school district, building-level school statistics, data on its library media center, and selected scores from the Iowa Tests of Basic Skills (ITBS) or the Tests of Achievement and Proficiency (TAP) (11).

Purpose:

The researchers report that this study sought to answer the following questions:

■ "Is there, in fact, a relationship between expenditures on LMCs [library media centers] and test performance, particularly when economic differences between communities and schools are controlled? Do test scores rise and fall with the fiscal fate of library media programs?

■ Assuming such a relationship, what characteristics of library media programs intervene to help to explain the relationship between expenditures on them and norm-referenced test scores? Can the number and level of LMC staff or the number of items or variety of formats in the collection be linked to test performance?

■ Does the performance of an instructional role by library media specialists help to predict norm-referenced test scores? Does the amount of collaboration between library media specialists and their colleagues in the classroom affect test performance?" (2)

Key Findings from the Initial Colorado Study:

- "The size of a library media center's staff and collection is the best school predictor of academic achievement.

- The instructional role of the library media specialist shapes the collection and, in turn, academic achievement.

- The degree of collaboration between library media specialists and teachers is affected by the ratio of teachers to pupils.

- Library media expenditures affect LMC staff and collection size and, in turn, academic achievement.

- Library media expenditures and staffing vary with total school expenditures and staffing.

- Among school and community predictors of academic achievement, the size of the LMC staff and collection is second only to the absence of at-risk conditions, particularly poverty and low educational attainment among adults" (92).

Used with permission from Keith Curry Lance.

Alaska, 1999

Lance, Keith Curry. *Information Empowered: The School Librarian as an Agent of Academic Achievement in Alaska Schools*.

Overview:

The Alaska State Library, in cooperation with the Alaska Department of Education and Early Development and the Institute for Social and Economic Research at the University of Alaska, Anchorage, contracted with the Colorado-based Library Research Service to perform this study. The study states:

"Library media centers from 211 Alaska public schools were surveyed about their staffing levels, hours of operation, staff activities, usage, technology, policies, and cooperation with public libraries. . . . For grades four, eight, and eleven, each school reported the percentage of students scoring below proficient, proficient, and above proficient on Version 5 of the California Achievement Tests (CAT5) of reading, language arts, and mathematics" (5).

Purpose:

Library media program characteristics were assessed as potential predictors of academic achievement, and their effects relative to other school and community factors were then analyzed (5).

This particular study focused on what the school librarian does during his day that positively impacts academic achievement. It is

> "an assessment of the impact of Alaska school librarians on academic achievement in the state's public schools. It examines the direct relationship between such staffing and student performance and identifies selected activities of library media staff that affect test scores. Other conditions of library media center operation—hours open, available technology, relationship with the public library, and selected policies—are also considered as potential predictors of academic achievement" (5).

Key Findings from the Alaska Study:

- ■ "Librarian Staffing: Where there is a librarian, test scores are higher. Generally, a school with a full-time librarian has higher test scores than a school with a part-time librarian. Accordingly, a school with a part-time librarian is likely to have higher test scores than a school with no librarian.

- ■ Library Media Center Hours Open: Higher levels of librarian staffing lead to longer LMC hours of operation, higher levels of library media staff activity, higher student usage, and consequently, higher test scores.

- ■ Staff Activities: The higher the level of librarian staffing, the greater the percentage of library media staff hours devoted to delivering library/information literacy instruction to students, planning instructional units cooperatively with teachers, and providing in-service training to teachers and other staff. Regardless of level of librarian staffing, the more library media staff time devoted to these activities, the higher the test scores.

- ■ Library Media Program Usage: The more often students receive library/information literacy instruction in which library media staff are involved, the higher the test scores.

- Partnerships, Technology, & Policies: Test scores also tend to be higher where there is a cooperative relationship between the LMC and the public library, the library media program provides online access to information—particularly the facilities required to reach the Internet and the World Wide Web—and the LMC has a collection development policy that addresses reconsideration of materials" (66–67).

Used with permission from Keith Curry Lance.

Pennsylvania, 2000

Lance, Keith Curry, Marcia J. Rodney, and Christine Hamilton-Pennell. *Measuring Up to Standards: The Impact of School Library Programs & Information Literacy in Pennsylvania Schools.*

Overview:

Pennsylvania Citizens for Better Libraries, the state's Friends of the Library group, in cooperation with the Pennsylvania Department of Education's Office of Commonwealth Libraries, contracted with the Colorado-based Library Research Service to perform this study. School library surveys were returned from 435 public schools. Pennsylvania System of School Assessment (PSSA) reading scores for fifth, eighth, and eleventh grades as well as other school and community factors were analyzed.

Purpose:

This study sought to "confirm in Pennsylvania the findings of the first Colorado study . . . [and] to expand on the original study's results by determining the impact on academic achievement of specific activities of certified school librarians; principal and teacher support of school library programs; and information technology, particularly licensed databases and the Internet/World Wide Web" (10).

Key Findings from the Pennsylvania Study:

- "Staffing: PSSA reading scores increase with increases in school librarian staff hours and support staff hours.

- Information Technology: Where networked computers link school libraries with classrooms, labs, and other instructional sites, students earn higher PSAA reading test scores. These higher scores are particularly linked to the numbers of computers enabling teachers and students to utilize the ACCESS PENNSYLVANIA database, licensed databases, and Internet/World Wide Web.

■ Integrating Information Literacy: The 'keystone' finding of this study is the importance of an integrated approach to information literacy. For school library programs to be successful agents of academic achievement, information literacy must be an integral part of the school's approach to both standards and curriculum. Test scores increase as school librarians spend more time:

> Teaching cooperatively with teachers;
> Teaching information literacy independently;
> Providing in-service training to teachers;
> Serving on standards committees;
> Serving on curriculum committees; and
> Managing information technology" (57–58).

Used with permission from Keith Curry Lance.

Colorado, 2000

Lance, Keith Curry, Marcia J. Rodney, and Christine Hamilton-Pennell. *How School Librarians Help Kids Achieve Standards: The Second Colorado Study.*

Overview:

In an effort to replicate and expand upon the 1993 Colorado study, researchers from the Library Research Service, Colorado State Library, Colorado Department of Education, and the Library and Information Services Department of the University of Denver joined together to conduct this second Colorado study. Surveys of school libraries were returned from 200 participating public schools. Data gathered were compared to fourth and seventh grade Colorado Student Assessment Program (CSAP) reading scores and analyzed against school and community conditions.

Purpose:

This study

> "reflects two new perspectives . . . First, it focuses atten tion on the library media specialist and the services he or she provides throughout the building, rather than just the

library media center as a specific place. Second, it emphasizes the fact that better library media services lead to better student performance on standards-based tests . . . It
measures the impact on academic achievement of specific
leadership and collaboration activities of library media
specialists, principal and teacher engagement in LM
[Library Media] programs, and information technology,
particularly networked computers offering licensed databases and the Internet/World Wide Web" (13).

Key Findings from the Second Colorado Study:

■ "Library Media Program Development: CSAP reading test
scores increase with increases in LMS hours per 100 students (7th grade), total staff hours per 100 students, print
volumes per student, periodical subscriptions per 100 students, electronic reference titles per 100 students (7th
grade), and library media expenditures per student.

■ Information Technology: Where networked computers link
library media centers with classrooms, labs, and other
instructional sites, students earn higher CSAP reading test
scores. These higher scores are particularly linked to the
numbers of computers enabling teachers and students to
utilize LMC resources, either within the LMC or networked to the LMC, licensed databases, and
Internet/World Wide Web.

■ Collaboration: A central finding of this study is the importance of a collaborative approach to information literacy.
Test scores rise in both elementary and middle schools as
library media specialists and teachers work together. In
addition, scores also increase with the amount of time
library media specialists spend as in-service trainers of
other teachers, acquainting them with the rapidly changing
world of information. Test scores increase as library media
specialists spend more time planning cooperatively with
teachers (7th grade), identifying materials for teachers,
teaching information literacy skills to students, providing
in-service training for teachers, managing a computer network through which the library media program reaches
beyond its own walls to classrooms, labs, and offices (7th
grade).

■ Flexible Scheduling: Students have greater freedom in
middle school and are often able to choose whether or not

they visit their school's LMC and use the resources there or take them home. Choosing to visit the LMC as an individual, separate from a class visit, is also a strong indicator of higher test scores. Middle schools with high test scores tend to have LMCs that report a high number of individual visits to the LMC on a per student basis" (77–78).

Used with permission from Keith Curry Lance.

Massachusetts, 2000

James C. Baughman. *School Libraries and MCAS Scores: A Paper Presented at a Symposium Sponsored by the Graduate School of Library and Information Science, Simmons College, Boston, Massachusetts.*

Overview and Purpose:

Concerned about the state of school libraries (the presence of a library within a school, staffed by a professional library media specialist, housing an adequate collection of up-to-date resources) in Massachusetts, James Baughman and Mary Eldringhoff conducted a statewide survey of public school libraries in order to provide baseline data. Surveys were returned from 519 of the state's public elementary, middle, and high school libraries. Data gathered were compared to combined scores in science, mathematics, and language arts on the Massachusetts Comprehensive Assessment System (MCAS) tests. The researchers also compared socioeconomic factors in the responding schools.

Key Findings from the Massachusetts Study:

- "At each grade level school library programs improve MCAS scores.

- At each grade level students score higher on MCAS tests when there is a higher per pupil book count.

- At each grade level students use of the library produces higher mean MCAS scores.

- At each grade level hours open make a difference in MCAS scores.

- At the elementary and middle/junior high school levels, students score higher on the MCAS tests when there is a library instruction program.

- At the elementary and middle/junior high school levels, average MCAS scores are higher in schools with larger per pupil expenditures for school library materials.

- At the elementary and high school levels, students who are served by a full-time school librarian have higher MCAS scores than those in schools without a full-time librarian.

- At the elementary and high school levels, library staff assistance (nonprofessional help) makes a positive difference in average MCAS scores.

- At the elementary level, students score higher on the MCAS tests when the library is aligned with the state curriculum frameworks. (This fact is especially true in schools that have a high percentage of free school lunches—the socioeconomic factor.)

- At the high school level, schools with automated collections have higher average MCAS scores" (8–9).

Used with permission from James C. Baughman.

Oregon, 2001

Lance, Keith Curry, Marcia J. Rodney, and Christine Hamilton-Pennell. *Good Schools Have School Librarians: Oregon School Librarians Collaborate to Improve Academic Achievement.*

Overview and Purpose:

The Oregon Educational Media Association, who with the Oregon State Library has been concerned about the condition of library media programs in Oregon public schools, contracted with the Colorado-based Library Research Service to conduct this study. The study states:

"In addition to confirming in Oregon the findings of the first Colorado study, this project also sought to explore several issues that were being explored in the other state studies. Those issues included identifying specific activities of library media staff that affect academic achievement, assessing the contribution of teacher and principal support of LM [library media] programs to the effectiveness of LM specialists, and examining the growing role of information technology in LM programs, particularly licensed databases and the Internet" (1).

Surveys of school library programs were returned from more than 500 participating public elementary, middle, and high schools in Oregon. Data for these schools were compared to Oregon Reading Scores for fifth, eighth, and tenth grades and analyzed against school differences and community differences.

Key Findings from the Oregon Study:

"Oregon reading test scores increase with increases in total staff hours per 100 students (including both professional and support staff), print volumes per student, periodical subscriptions per 100 students, and library media expenditures per student. Whatever the current level of development of a school's library media program, these findings indicate that incremental improvements in its staffing, collections, and budget will yield incremental increases in reading scores" (83).

Used with permission from Keith Curry Lance.

Texas, 2001

Smith, Ester G. *Texas School Libraries: Standards, Resources, Services, and Students' Performance*, prepared by E.G.S. Research and Consulting for the Texas State Library and Archives Commission, April 2002.

Overview and Purpose:

The Texas Study had three objectives:

"(1) Examine school library resources, services, and use on the basis of the 'School Library Programs: Standards and Guidelines for Texas' and determine the need for updating these standards and guidelines so that they better serve communities across the State. (2) Determine the impact that school libraries have on student performance as measured by the percent of students who met minimum expectations on the reading portion of the statewide standardized test, the Texas Assessment of Academic Skills (TAAS). (3) Highlight library practices in the best-performing schools" (1).

Surveys were returned from 503 public elementary, middle, and high school libraries, an 84% return rate from the 600 school libraries that had been randomly selected. Data were then compared to student performance on the Texas Assessment of Academic Skills test at the fourth, eighth, and tenth grade levels.

Key Findings from the Texas Study:

"The Texas Study demonstrated higher TAAS performance at all educational levels in schools with librarians than in schools without librarians . . . The Texas Study also showed that socio-economic variables such as the percentage of white students, Hispanic students, and economically disadvantaged students explain most of the variance in TAAS performance at all educational levels . . . Library variables explained a smaller but still very significant portion of the variance in TAAS performance . . . Also, library variables were generally more important to explaining the variance in TAAS than school variables such as the number of school computers per student, teacher experience, and teacher turnover ratio" (1–2).

"Library variables found to be important were:

Elementary School:

- Library volumes purchased in 1999–2000 per 100 students
- Library operational expenditures per student
- Library computers connected to a modem per 100 students
- Library software packages per 100 students

Middle/Junior High School:

- Identifying materials for instructional units developed by teachers
- Providing information skills instruction to individuals or groups

High School:

- Library staff per 100 students
- Library staff hours per 100 students
- Library hours of operation per 100 students
- Volumes per student
- Current subscription to magazines and newspapers per 100 students

- Planning instructional units with teachers
- Providing staff development to teachers" (2)

Reprinted with permission of the Library Development Division of the Texas State Library.

Iowa, 2002

Rodney, Marcia J., Keith Curry Lance, and Christine Hamilton-Pennell. *Make the Connection: Quality School Library Media Programs Impact Academic Achievement in Iowa.*

Overview and Purpose:

The Iowa AEAs (Area Education Agencies) directed this research project to "document the impact of LM [library media] programs in Iowa schools and to share this information with school decision-makers for library media programs—school boards, superintendents, principals, teachers, even library media specialists" (1). Data collected from 506 elementary, middle, and high schools were compared with fourth and eighth grade reading scores on the Iowa Tests for Basic Skills and with eleventh grade reading scores on the Iowa Tests of Educational Development. School and community factors were also analyzed.

Key Findings from the Iowa Study:

Reading test scores in grades four, eight, and eleven are positively impacted by the following:

- The presence of at least one full-time, professionally trained and credentialed library media specialist (39);

- The size of the collection and the availability and accessibility of the collection to students (42–44);

- The library media specialist "planning instructional units with teachers, providing-inservice training to teachers, attending faculty meetings, working on standards and curriculum committees, and teaching cooperatively with classroom teachers" (47).

Used with permission from Keith Curry Lance.

Appendix B
Sample Planning and Unit Evaluation Forms

Collaborative Unit Planning Sheet

*Teacher:*_____
(could be teachers; teams)

*Library media specialist:*_____

Content area:_____   **Unit of study:**_____
(could be interdisciplinary)

Unit planning began (date):_____   **Unit ended (date):**_____

Goals and objectives of the unit:

_____

_____

Proposed learning activities and products:

_____

_____

Responsibilities: (for each, mark T=Teacher; LMS=Library Media Specialist; SP=Specialist; A=All)

_____

_____

How will we assess learning?

_____

_____

What happened? (list activities as they occur)
Example: mini-lesson on how to judge currency of information (teacher and LMS taught)

_____

_____

Reprinted with permission from Loertscher, David V. *Taxonomies of the School Library Media Program*, 2nd ed.

Teacher/Library Media Specialist Evaluation of a Collaboratively Taught Unit

(TO BE FILLED IN AS A TEAM)

Unit Title:_____

Total time spent by LMS:_____ **# Students affected:**_____

What worked well in the unit?_____

_____

Suggestions for improvement:_____

_____

What information skills were integrated into the unit?
(Time spent by LMS:)(as a subset of the total time listed above)

_____

_____

From both the teacher's and the library media specialist's points of view, was this unit enhanced through collaboration?   Yes   No   Why?

_____

_____

Was the unit successful enough to warrant doing it again in the future?
Yes   No   Why?

_____

_____

How well did the library collection respond to the unit objectives?
Scale: 5=excellent; 4=above average; 3=average; 2=below average; 1=poor

- ❏ Diversity of formats (books, audiovisual, electronic)
- ❏ Recency (books and other materials up to date)
- ❏ Duplication (enough materials for the number of students taught)
- ❏ Reading/viewing/listening levels meeting students' needs
- ❏ Average of above ratings

What materials/technology will we need if we are planning to repeat the unit again?

_____

_____

Reprinted with permission from Loertscher, David V. *Taxonomies of the School Library Media Program*, 2nd ed.

Appendix C
Sample Pathfinders

Prince Edward County Elementary School Library
Pathfinder on Ancient Greece

Third Grade History SOL

Catalog Search

To conduct a search using "Athena," our automated card catalog, go to a computer workstation and double click on the purple Athena icon on the desktop screen. Type in one or more of the suggested keywords below in the search box, and then click on "search" on the right side of the screen. The list of items that Athena shows are items available in our school library.

Suggested keywords:

Greece	Greeks
Ancient Greece	Civilization

Books Available in Our Library

Ancient Greece (country)

- Pearson, Anne. *Ancient Greece*. 1994. New York: D.K. Publishing.
- Neurath, Marie. *They Lived Like This in Ancient Greece*. 1968. New York: F. Watts Publishing.
- Forrest, Martin. *Ancient Greece*. 1992. Crystal Lake, IL: Rigby.* (11 copies)

* Denotes multiple copies (novel set) for use in classroom.

Ancient Greeks (people)

- Horton, Casey. *Ancient Greeks*. 1984. New York: Gloucester Press.
- Odijk, Pamela. *The Greeks*. 1989. Englewood, NJ: Silver Burdett.
- Taylor, Pat. *The Ancient Greeks*. 1997. Crystal Lake, IL: Heinemann Press.
- Kerr, Daisy. *Ancient Greeks*. 1997. New York: F. Watts Publishing.

Folktales of Ancient Greece

- Neufeld, Rose. *Beware the Man Without a Beard*. 1969. New York: Knopf Publishing.

Mythology of Greece

- Bullfinch, Thomas. *Mythology*. 1970. New York: Crowell Publishing.
- Elgin, Kathleen. *The First Book of Mythology*. 1955. New York: F. Watts Publishing.
- Witting, Alisoun. *Treasury of Greek Mythology*. 1966. New York: Harvey House.

continued

Biography
 • Green, Robert. *Alexander the Great*. 1996. New York: F. Watts Publishing.

Reference Books in Our Library

Children's Atlas of Civilizations. 1994. Brookfield, CT: Millbrook Press.

Atlas of Ancient Worlds. 1994. New York: D. K. Publishing.

World Book Encyclopedia. 1998. Chicago: World Book.

Online Reference Sources (in library)

Encyclopedia Britannica Online (shortcut icon on workstation desktop)

World Book Online (shortcut icon on workstation desktop)

SIRS Discoverer (shortcut icon on workstation desktop)

Other Sources Available in Our Library

"Ancient Greece" Vertical File Folder
 • Contains puzzles, visual aids, fact sheets, and games. Available in the top drawer of the red file cabinet under "G."

Transparency Pack
 • Contains a visual library of images for use on overheads. Includes transparencies on everyday life of Greeks, geography of Greece, battle maps, etc.
 • Available in the black binder on the A/V cart. Please bring to circulation desk for checkout.

Internet Sites

http://members.aol.com/Donnclass/Greeklife.html
Wonderful interactive, student friendly site containing games and many visuals. Includes info on Greek customs, clothing, occupations and hobbies.

http://www.mrdowling.com/701greece.html
A Sylvan Learning Center website that includes basic history and geography of Greece. Other topics include Athens, Socrates, mythology and Alexander the Great.

http://www.arwhead.com/Greeks/
This site covers all aspects of Greek life. Information is supplied about topics such as art and music of Greece, the roles of men and women in Greece and the organization of Greek government.

http://www.richmond.edu/~ed344/webunits/greecerome/civ.html
A "safesurf" rated site that contains information on the 2 civilizations of Greece and Rome. Designed as an introduction for third grade students. This site covers the Standard of Learning 3.1 of the Virginia History SOL.

Pathfinder Designed by Angela M. Moore, 2002.

Sample Pathfinder, Prince Edward County Elementary School Library, Farmville, Virginia, reprinted with permission from Angela M. Moore.

Manchester High School Library
Portfolio Project—Sub-Saharan Africa

Project Pathfinder—Ms. Hebert, Mr. Long, Ms. Szwabowski

Current Events (region):

- ProQuest Direct - Online Magazine and Newspaper Database. (See a library media specialist for information about home access.)
- LINC: Chesterfield County Public Library Catalog - (Select "Electronic Resources" from the LINC home page. Access requires Chesterfield County library card. The database "EbscoMasterFile" is another magazine database. See media specialist for more information.)
- SIRS Knowledge Source
- Print news sources available in the MHS Library include:
  Richmond Times-Dispatch
  USA Today
  Time Magazine
  Newsweek Magazine
  U.S. News and World Report

Internet Sites:
CNN

MSNBC

ABC NEWS

BBC NEWS

USA TODAY

Economic Development Indicators (countries)

Standard of Living and Quality of Life Indicators (countries)

Political Characteristics (region and countries)

Social Characteristics (region)

Books (Regular and Reference):
Suggested Subjects for Library Catalog
(to find books and other library materials)

Subject Search: Name of individual country
Keyword Search: Name of individual country

Print **encyclopedia sets** are located in the reference section.

Reference resources include:

R 910 Wor *World Factbook*
On-line World Factbook

R 317.3 Wor *World Almanac*
On-line World Almanac as part of SIRS Knowledge

R 390 Cul *Culturgrams*

R 305.8 Wor *Worldmark Encyclopedia of Cultures and Daily Life*
R 910.22 Lan *Lands and People*
On-line Lands and People

continued

R 304.6 Nes *Encyclopedia of Global Population and Demographics*

R 301 Wor *World Quality Of Life Indicators*

R 916 Afr *Africa*

R 305.896 Enc *Encyclopedia of African Peoples*

Other Reference Sources:
- Groliers Encyclopedia Online. (See a library media specialist for information about home access.)
  Includes:
  Encyclopedia Americana
  Grolier Multimedia Encyclopedia
  New Book of Knowledge
  Lands and People
- *World Book Multimedia Encyclopedia* - CD-ROM
- *Colliers Encyclopedia* - CD-ROM

Additional Internet Sites:
Information Please Almanac

Chiefs of State

CountryWatch

World Area Studies Internet Resources

African Links

Africa - South of the Sahara

African Studies - Internet Resources

Library of Congress Country Studies

Religious Population of the World

Ethnologue: languages of the world

Discussion of Country:
R 338.9 Hum *Human Development Report*
(includes the Human Development Index formulas and tables)
On-line Human Development Report

R 390 Cul *Culturgrams* (includes the Human Development Index rating)

Citing Sources:
MHS Library Media Center's Sample Works-Cited Entries (MLA) - Examples are taken from resources available in the Manchester High School Library Media Center.

MLA Citation Style Guide (Traditional Sources)

EasyBib - This bibliography generator allows you to complete a form for each source you use. It generates an MLA works-cited entry based on the information you give it.

Pathfinder created by Catherine Welsh/Lois Stanton. *Last modified 04/11/2002.*

Sample Pathfinder, Manchester High School Library, Midlothian, Virginia, reprinted with permission from Catherine Welsh and Lois Stanton.

Appendix D
Principal Brochures, Virginia Department of Education

A Guide for Elementary School Principals

Academic Success @your library™

Powerful Partnerships: Your School Librarian and YOU!

Come to the library where Information is SOL Power

Virginia Department of Education
Office of Instructional Media and Training
P.O. Box 2120
Richmond, VA 23218-2120

Key Resources

Virginia Department of Education Web pages
http://www.pen.k12.va.us/VDOE/Technology/imtresources.htm#librarymedia

Guide for Developing and Evaluating School Library Media Programs, 6th Edition (Nebraska Educational Media Association, Libraries Unlimited, Englewood, CO, 2000)

*Information Power: Building Partnerships for Learning (American Library Association, Chicago, 1998)

Library Research Service
http://www.lrs.org/

Literacy Partners: A Principal's Guide To An Effective Library Media Program For the 21st Century (Alabama Department of Education, c. 1999)

Taxonomies of the School Library Media Program, 2nd edition (David V. Loertscher, Hi Willow Publishing, San Jose, CA, 2000)

Virginia Educational Media Association Web pages
http://www.vema.gen.va.us

Need Direction?

Ask A Librarian.

For additional information contact:
Charlie Makela
804-786-9412
Cmakela@pen.k12.va.us

Can you find these @your library™?

➤ Licensed librarian
➤ Library support staff
➤ Students engaged in learning
➤ Welcoming atmosphere
➤ A current book collection
➤ Recreational reading opportunities
➤ Brochures, bookmarks, and style sheets on display
➤ New materials on display
➤ Locations of materials clearly marked
➤ Sufficient, functional technology tools
➤ Space arranged for group and/or individual use
➤ Alternative scheduling options for the library
➤ Evidence of collaborative lesson planning
➤ Opportunities exist for student and teacher input into the library program
➤ Library's mission statement is visible

Reprinted with permission from the Virginia Department of Education, Office of Educational Technology.

Essential Elements for Elementary School Library Programs

For a successful program, discuss these elements with your librarian.

Learning and Teaching

Studies prove a direct correlation between student achievement on standardized tests and a dynamic library program.*

Goal: The library program is integral to Virginia Standards of Learning (SOL) success.

Key Question:
➤ What opportunities do students have to access, use, and evaluate information for SOL success?

Goal: Students are actively involved in learning activities.

Key Question:
➤ How does the library program inspire students to read, write, and use resources effectively and enthusiastically?

Goal: Librarians and teachers are involved in lesson collaboration.

Key Question:
➤ When is time available for the teachers and librarians to work together to plan lessons based on the SOL?

Goal: The current collection supports curriculum needs.

Key Questions:
➤ What print and electronic materials support the instructional needs of the students?
➤ Does the library have adequate equipment to support the needs of teachers and students?
➤ Does the collection meet the Virginia Standards of Accreditation (SOA) criteria?

Goal: The "library ... program encourages and engages students in reading, viewing, and listening for understanding and enjoyment" (AASL, p 58)*.

Key Question:
➤ What activities does the library foster to promote reading and learning?

Information Access and Delivery

Successful student-centered library programs depend on flexible access and collaboration with teachers.*

Goal: Students have access to information.

Key Questions:
➤ What strategies does the library program provide to help students find information in all formats?
➤ Are electronic resources operational?
➤ How physically accessible are all library resources to students and teachers?

Goal: The climate is conducive to learning.

Key Question:
➤ How does the library convey an inviting atmosphere that provides optimal lighting, noise level, and temperature?

Goal: There is flexible and equitable access to resources.

Key Questions:
➤ Which resources can be accessed from classrooms and from home?
➤ How consistently is the library available for SOL-based instructional use?

Goal: There is ongoing collection development and evaluation of the library program.

Key Question:
➤ How and when are resources continually updated to meet the SOL?

Goal: There is a commitment to intellectual freedom.

Key Question:
➤ What and where are the written policies for selecting resources and handling challenged materials?

Goal: Legal and ethical use of resources is demonstrated.

Key Question:
➤ What information does the library provide about resource citation and copyright issues?

Program Administration

Well-managed library programs require adequate staffing, funding, and administrative support.*

Goal: The library program supports the goals and improvement of the school.

Key Question:
➤ How often is the librarian included in goal setting and school improvement planning?

Goal: Professional and support staff is available in the library.

Key Question:
➤ Does the staffing meet the Virginia Standards of Accreditation (SOA)?

Goal: There is evidence of effective management of the library.

Key Questions:
➤ How are SOL test data, resource guides, and local curriculum guides used to develop the library program?
➤ What documentation (circulation statistics, collection additions, library schedule/plan book, and number of classes served) is available to support the library program?

Goal: There is strong administrative support.

Key Question:
➤ How does the building administration support the library's budget, staffing, and scheduling for a quality program?

Goal: Professional development is ongoing.

Key Question:
➤ What opportunities does the librarian have to participate in local, state, and national professional growth activities?

Goal: Staff development is ongoing.

Key Question:
➤ What instruction does the library provide in the use of resources and technology using established best practices?

Reprinted with permission from the Virginia Department of Education, Office of Educational Technology.

Essential Elements for Middle School Library Programs

For a successful program, discuss these elements with your librarian.

Learning and Teaching

Studies prove a direct correlation between student achievement on standardized tests and a dynamic library program. *

Goal: The library program is integral to Virginia Standards of Learning (SOL) success.
Key Question:
➤ When is time provided for teachers and librarians to collaboratively plan lessons that support the SOL?

Goal: Students are actively involved in learning activities.
Key Question:
➤ How are students using available resources?

Goal: There is development of information literacy skills within the library program.
Key Question:
➤ Which learning activities teach users to find, evaluate and use information responsibly and effectively?

Goal: The collection is current and supportive of curriculum.
Key Questions:
➤ What print and electronic resources meet instructional needs?
➤ How routinely are these resources used?
➤ How much equipment is available to meet curriculum needs?
➤ Does the collection meet the Virginia Standards of Accreditation (SOA) criteria?

Goal: There is involvement in curriculum planning.
Key Question:
➤ How often is the librarian involved in meeting department heads, curriculum planning, school improvement, and other initiatives?

Information Access and Delivery

Successful student-centered library programs depend on flexible access and collaboration with teachers. *

Goal: Students have access to information.
Key Questions:
➤ What strategies does the library program provide to help students and teachers use all types of information resources?
➤ Are electronic resources operational?
➤ How physically accessible are all library resources to students and teachers?

Goal: The climate is conducive to learning.
Key Question:
➤ How inviting is the library with regard to optimal lighting, noise level, and temperature?

Goal: There is flexible and equitable access to resources.
Key Questions:
➤ Which resources can be accessed from classrooms and from home?
➤ How consistently is the library available for SOL-based instructional use?

Goal: There is ongoing collection development and evaluation of the library program.
Key Questions:
➤ How and when are resources continually updated to meet the SOL?
➤ How do the teachers and librarian collaborate to provide a current and appropriate collection?

Goal: Legal and ethical use of resources is demonstrated.
Key Questions:
➤ What information does the library provide about resource citation and copyright issues?
➤ What and where are the written policies for selecting resources and handling challenged materials?

Program Administration

Well-managed library programs require adequate staffing, funding, and administrative support. *

Goal: The library program supports the goals and improvement of the school.
Key Question:
➤ How often is the librarian included in goal setting and school improvement planning?

Goal: Professional and support staff are available in the library.
Key Question:
➤ Does the staffing meet the Virginia Standards of Accreditation (SOA)?

Goal: There is evidence of effective management of the library.
Key Questions:
➤ How are SOL test data, resource guides, and local curriculum guides used to develop the library program?
➤ What documentation such as circulation statistics, collection additions, library schedule/plan book, and number of classes served is available to support the library program?

Goal: There is strong administrative support.
Key Question:
➤ How does the building administration support the library's budget, staffing, and scheduling for a quality program?

Goal: Professional development is ongoing.
Key Question:
➤ What opportunities does the librarian have to participate in local, state, and national conferences?

Goal: There is ongoing staff development.
Key Question:
➤ What instruction does the library provide in the use of resources and technology using established best practices?

A Guide for Secondary School Principals

Academic Success
@your library

Powerful Partnerships:
Your School Librarian
and
YOU!

Come to the library
where **Information** is
SOL Power

Virginia Department of Education
Office of Instructional Media and Training
P.O. Box 2120
Richmond, VA 23218-2120

Key Resources

Virginia Department of Education Web pages
http://www.pen.k12.va.us/VDOE/Technology/imresources.htm#librarymedia

Guide for Developing and Evaluating School Library Media Programs, 6th Edition (Nebraska Educational Media Association, Libraries Unlimited, Englewood, CO, 2000)

*Information Power: Building Partnerships for Learning (American Library Association, Chicago, 1998)

Library Research Service
http://www.lrs.org/

Literacy Partners: A Principal's Guide To An Effective Library Media Program For the 21st Century (Alabama Department of Education, c. 1999)

Taxonomies of the School Library Media Program, 2nd edition (David V. Loertscher, Hi Willow Publishing, San Jose, CA, 2000)

Virginia Educational Media Association Web pages
http://www.vema.gen.va.us

Need Direction?

Ask A Librarian.

For additional information contact:
Charlie Makela
804-786-9412
Cmakela@pen.k12.va.us

Can you find these @ your library ?

- Licensed librarian
- Library support staff
- Students engaged in learning
- Welcoming atmosphere
- A current book collection
- Recreational reading opportunities
- Brochures, bookmarks, and style sheets on display
- New materials on display
- Locations of materials clearly marked
- Sufficient, functional technology tools
- Space arranged for group and/or individual use
- Evidence of collaborative planning for instruction
- Opportunities exist for student and teacher input to the library program
- Library mission statement visible

Reprinted with permission from the Virginia Department of Education, Office of Educational Technology.

Essential Elements for Secondary School Library Programs

For a successful program, discuss these elements with your librarian.

Learning and Teaching

Studies prove a direct correlation between student achievement on standardized tests and a dynamic library program. *

Goal: The library program is integral to Virginia Standards of Learning (SOL) success.
Key Question:
▶ When is time provided for teachers and librarians to collaboratively plan lessons that support the SOL?

Goal: Students are actively involved in learning activities.
Key Question:
▶ How are students using available resources?

Goal: There is development of information literacy skills within the library program.
Key Questions:
▶ Which learning activities teach users to find, evaluate and use information responsibly and effectively?

Goal: The collection is current and supportive of curriculum.
Key Questions:
▶ What print and electronic resources meet instructional needs?
▶ How routinely are these resources used?
▶ How much equipment is available to meet curriculum needs?
▶ Does the collection meet the Virginia Standards of Accreditation (SOA) criteria?

Goal: There is involvement in curriculum planning.
Key Question:
▶ How often is the librarian involved in meeting department heads, curriculum planning, school improvement, and other initiatives?

Information Access and Delivery

Successful student-centered library programs depend on flexible access and collaboration with teachers. *

Goal: Students have access to information.
Key Questions:
▶ What strategies does the library program provide to help students and teachers use all types of information resources?
▶ Are electronic resources operational?
▶ How physically accessible are all library resources to students and teachers?

Goal: The climate is conducive to learning.
Key Question:
▶ How inviting is the library with regard to optimal lighing, noise level, and temperature?

Goal: There is flexible and equitable access to resources.
Key Questions:
▶ Which resources can be accessed from classrooms and from home?
▶ How consistently is the library available for SOL-based instructional use?

Goal: There is ongoing collection development and evaluation of the library program.
Key Questions:
▶ How and when are resources continually updated to meet the SOL and the SOA?
▶ Does the library budget provide for ongoing collection development?

Goal: Legal and ethical use of resources is demonstrated and practiced.
Key Questions:
▶ What information does the library provide about resource citation and copyright issues?
▶ What and where are the written policies for selecting resources and handling challenged materials?

Program Administration

Well-managed library programs require adequate staffing, funding, and administrative support. *

Goal: The library program supports the goals and improvement of the school.
Key Question:
▶ How often is the librarian included in goal setting and school improvement planning?

Goal: Professional and support staff are available in the library.
Key Question:
▶ Does the staffing meet the Virginia Standards of Accreditation (SOA)?

Goal: There is evidence of effective management of the library.
Key Questions:
▶ How are SOL test data, resource guides, and local curriculum guides used to develop the library program?
▶ What documentation is available such as circulation statistics, collection additions, library schedule/plan book, and number of classes served to support the library program?

Goal: There is strong administrative support.
Key Question:
▶ How does the building administration support the library's budget, staffing, and scheduling for a quality program?

Goal: Professional development is ongoing.
Key Question:
▶ What opportunities does the librarian have to participate in local, state, and national professional growth activities?

Goal: There is ongoing staff development.
Key Question:
▶ What instruction does the library provide to staff in the use of resources and technology using established best practices?

References

Baughman, James C. *School Libraries and MCAS Scores: A Paper Presented at a Symposium Sponsored by the Graduate School of Library and Information Science, Simmons College, Boston, Massachusetts. 26 October 2000.* 15 May 2002 <http://web.simmons.edu/~baughman/mcas-school-libraries/>.

Carleton, Fran. Personal interview. 25 Sept. 2002.

Clemons, C. Rodney. Personal interview. 19 Aug. 2002.

Cohen, Laura. *Boolean Searching on the Internet.* May 2002. University at Albany Libraries. 14 May 2002 <http://library.albany.edu/internet/boolean.html>.

Edwards, Mark A. "Evolution of the Library." *VEMA Mediagram* 26.3 (2001): 4.

Eisenberg, Michael B. *The Big6 Skills Overview.* 25 November 2002 <http://www.big6.com/showarticle.php?id=16>.

Eisenberg, Michael B. and Robert E. Berkowitz. *Information Problem-Solving: The Big6 Skills Approach to Library and Information Skills Instruction.* Norwood, NJ: Ablex, 1990.

Everhart, Nancy. *Evaluating the School Library Media Center: Analysis Techniques and Research Practices.* Englewood, CO: Libraries Unlimited, 1998.

Hartzell, Gary N. *Building Influence for the School Librarian.* Worthington, OH: Linworth, 1994.

—-. "The Invisible School Librarian." *School Library Journal* Nov. 1997: 24–29.

—-. *What's It Take?* IMLS: Publications Conferences & Resources: Conferences 4 June 2002. 23 Jan. 2003 <http://www.imls.gov/pubs/whitehouse0602/garyhartzell.htm>.

Hughes-Hassell, Sandra and Anne Wheelock, eds. *The Information-Powered School.* Chicago: American Library Association, 2001.

Information Power: Building Partnerships for Learning. Chicago: American Library Association, 1998.

Jenkins, Bob. Personal interview. 5 Sept. 2002.

Johnson, Doug. *The Indispensable Librarian: Surviving (and Thriving) in School Media Centers in the Information Age.* Worthington, OH: Linworth, 1997.

Jones, Angela. Personal interview. 7 Nov. 2002.

Krashen, Stephen. "What Do We Know About Libraries and Reading Achievement? Access to Books=More Reading=More Reading Achievement." *Book Report* Jan./Feb. 2002: 38.

Kuhlthau, Carol Collier. *Seeking Meaning: A Process Approach to Library and Information Services.* Norwood, NJ: Ablex, 1993.

Lance, Keith Curry et al. *Information Empowered: The School Librarian as an Agent of Academic Achievement in Alaska Schools.* Juneau: Alaska State Library, 1999.

Lance, Keith Curry, Marcia J. Rodney, and Christine Hamilton-Pennell. *Good Schools Have School Librarians: Oregon School Librarians Collaborate to Improve Academic Achievement.* [n.p.]: Oregon Educational Media Association, 2001.

Lance, Keith Curry, Marcia J. Rodney, and Christine Hamilton-Pennell. *How School Librarians Help Kids Achieve Standards: The Second Colorado Study.* San Jose, CA: HiWillow, 2000.

Lance, Keith Curry, Marcia J. Rodney, and Christine Hamilton-Pennell. *Measuring Up to Standards: The Impact of School Library Programs & Information Literacy in Pennsylvania Schools.* 2000. 15 May 2002 <http://www.statelibrary.state.pa.us/libraries/lib/libraries/measuringup.pdf>.

Lance, Keith Curry, Lynda Welborn, and Christine Hamilton-Pennell. *The Impact of School Library Media Centers on Academic Achievement.* Castle Rock, CO: HiWillow, 1993.

Laura Bush Foundation for America's Libraries. *Washington White House Conference on School Libraries Checks Out Lessons for Success.* 4 June 2002. 13 August 2002 <http://www.laurabushfoundation.org/release_060402.html>.

Loertscher, David V. *Collection Mapping in the LMC: Building Access in a World of Technology.* San Jose, CA: HiWillow, 1996.

—-. *Reinvent Your School's Library in the Age of Technology: A Guide for Principals and Superintendents*. San Jose, CA: HiWillow, 1998.

—-. *Taxonomies of the School Library Media Program*. 2nd ed. San Jose, CA: HiWillow, 2000.

Lowe, Karen R. *Resource Alignment: Providing Curriculum Support in the School Library Media Center*. Millers Creek, NC: Beacon Consulting, 2001.

Manzo, Kathleen Kennedy. "Study Shows Rise in Test Scores Tied to School Library Resources." 22 March 2000. *Education Week on the Web*. 27 February 2002 <http://www.educationweek.org/ew/ewstory.cfm?slug=28libe.h19>.

Martin, Ann M. Personal interview. 3 Sept. 2002.

McKenzie, Jamie. *Beyond Technology: Questioning, Research, and the Information Literate School*. Bellingham, WA: FNO Press, 2000.

Miller, Marilyn. "Information Power: Building Partnerships for Learning." *Knowledge Quest* Sept./Oct. 1998: 14–18.

Miller, Marilyn and Marilyn Shontz. "New Money, Old Books." *School Library Journal* Oct. 2001: 50–60.

OCLC Forest Press. "About Dewey: Second Summary." *Dewey Decimal Classification*. 23 Jan. 2003 <http://www.oclc.org/dewey/about/hundreds.htm>.

Pennock, Robin. "Trading Places: A Librarian's Route to the Principal's Office." *School Library Journal* Sept. 1988: 117–119.

Perritt, Patsy H. "Getting Certified in 50 States: The Latest Requirements for School Librarians." *School Library Journal* June 2000: 50–72.

Pharr, Faye. *Reflections of an Empowered Library*. IMLS: Publications Conferences & Resources: Conferences 5 June 2002. 23 Jan. 2003 <http://www.imls.gov/pubs/whitehouse0602/fayepharr.htm>.

Price, Joyce. Personal interview. 6 Nov. 2002.

Robinson, Mary. Personal interview. 3 Sept. 2002.

Rodney, Marcia J., Keith Curry Lance, and Christine Hamilton-Pennell. *Make the Connection: Quality School Library Media Programs Impact Academic Achievement in Iowa*. Bettendorf, IA: Mississippi Bend Area Education Agency, 2002.

Simpson, Carol. *Copyright for Schools: A Practical Guide*. Worthington, OH: Linworth, 2001.

"Thus Said." *American Libraries* August 2002: 41.

Smith, Ester G. *Texas School Libraries: Standards, Resources, Services, and Students' Performance*. April 2001. 15 May 2002 <http://www.tsl.state.tx.us/ld/pubs/schlibsurvey/index.html>.

Standards of Learning for Virginia Public Schools. Richmond, VA: Board of Education, 1995.

Todd, Ross. *Transitions for Preferred Futures of School Libraries: Knowledge Space, Not Information Place; Connections, Not Collections; Actions, Not Positions; Evidence, Not Advocacy*. International Association of School Librarianship Conference, Auckland, New Zealand, July 9–12, 2001. 11 August 2002 <http://www.iasl-slo.org/virtualpaper2001.html>.

Van De Mortell, Paul. Personal interview. 5 Sept. 2002.

Van Metre Tate, Julie. Personal interview. 27 Aug. 2002.

Wheelock, Anne. *Executive Summary: Findings from the Evaluation of the National Library Power Program*. 15 May 2002 <http://www.wallacefunds.org/lila/publications/pdf/libpowr.pdf>.

Yucht, Alice H. *Flip It! An Information Skills Strategy for Student Researchers*. Worthington, OH: Linworth, 1997.

For Further Reading

Alexander, Jan and Marsha Tate. *Evaluating Web Resources.* 25 July
2001. Wolfgram Memorial Library, Widener University.
14 May 2002 <http://www2.widener.edu/
Wolfgram-Memorial-Library/webevaluation/webeval.htm>.

American Association of School Librarians. *A Planning Guide for
Information Power: Building Partnerships for Learning with
School Library Media Program Assessment Rubric for the 21st
Century.* Chicago: American Association of School Librarians,
American Library Association, 1999.

Black, Susan. "Reading Room: Today's School Libraries Are Bustling
Centers of Learning." *ASBJ.com.* February 2001. 27 February
2002 <http://www.asbj.com/2001/02/0201research.html>.

Bush, Gail. *The Principal's Manual for Your School Library Media
Program.* 27 February 2002
<http://www.ala.org/aasl/principalsmanual.html>.

Buzzeo, Toni. *Collaborating to Meet Standards: Teacher/Librarian
Partnerships for K–6.* Worthington, OH: Linworth, 2002.

Doiron, Ray and Judy Davies. *Partners in Learning: Students, Teachers,
and the School Library.* Englewood, CO: Libraries Unlimited,
1998.

Donham, Jean. *Enhancing Teaching and Learning: A Leadership Guide
for School Library Media Specialists.* New York: Neal-Schuman,
1998.

Donham, Jean et al. *Inquiry-Based Learning: Lessons from Library
Power.* Worthington, OH: Linworth, 2001.

Haycock, Ken. "Fostering Collaboration, Leadership and Information
Literacy: Common Behaviors of Uncommon Principals and
Faculties." *NASSP Bulletin* March 1999: 82–87.

Lance, Keith Curry and David V. Loertscher. *Powering Achievement:
School Library Media Programs Make a Difference: The
Evidence.* San Jose, CA: HiWillow, 2001.

Library Power: Strategies for Teaching and Learning in America's Public Schools. 15 May 2002 <http://www.wallacefunds.org/publications/pub_library/index.htm>.

"Literacy Partners: A Principal's Guide to an Effective Library Media Program for the 21st Century." [n.p.]: Alabama Department of Education, 1999.

Loertscher, David V. and Douglas Achterman. *Increasing Academic Achievement Through the Library Media Center: A Guide for Teachers.* Castle Rock, CO: HiWillow, 2002.

Loupe, Diane. "Libraries and Technology: Even in the Internet Age, What Matters Most Are Good People and Good Content." *eSchool News Online.* 01 Nov. 2001. 27 February 2002 <http://www.eschoolnews.com/resources/reports/libraries1101/>.

Powerful Partnerships Your School Librarian and You: Come to the Library Where Information Is SOL Power! Virginia Department of Education. 11 August 2002 <http://www.pen.k12.va.us/VDOE/Technology/imtresources.html#librarymedia>.

Schrock, Kathy. *Critical Evaluation Information.* 14 May 2002 <http://school.discovery.com/schrockguide/eval.html>.

Simpson, Carol. *Copyright for Schools: A Practical Guide.* Worthington, OH: Linworth, 2001.

Zweizig, Douglas L. and Dianne McAfee Hopkins. *Lessons from Library Power: Enriching Teaching and Learning.* Englewood, CO: Libraries Unlimited, 1999.

Index

S

T

V

W

About the Author

Audrey Puckett Church was a building-level library media specialist in Virginia public schools for 20 years. Currently she coordinates and teaches in the graduate program in school library media at Longwood University in Farmville, Virginia. A frequent presenter at regional, state, and national conferences, she is past president of her state professional organization, the Virginia Educational Media Association, and past secretary of the Educators of Library Media Specialists Section of the American Association of School Librarians. She believes passionately, as the research shows, that school libraries and school librarians significantly impact student achievement.